ROCK ON

How I Tried to Stop Caring about Music
and Learn to Love Corporate Rock

DAN KENNEDY

LIMERICK
COUNTY LIBRARY

00571991

781
66...

Harvill *Secker*
LONDON

Published by Harvill Secker 2008

First published in the United States in 2008 by Algonquin Books

2 4 6 8 10 9 7 5 3 1

Copyright © Dan Kennedy 2008

Dan Kennedy has asserted his right under the Copyright,
Designs and Patents Act 1988 to be identified as the author of this work

This book is sold subject to the condition that it shall not, by way of trade
or otherwise, be lent, resold, hired out, or otherwise circulated without
the publisherís prior consent in any form of binding or cover other than
that in which it is published and without a similar condition, including
this condition, being imposed on the subsequent purchaser.

First published in Great Britain in 2008 by
Harvill Secker

Random House, 20 Vauxhall Bridge Road,
London SW1V 2SA

www.rbooks.co.uk

Addresses for companies within The Random House Group Limited can
be found at: www.randomhouse.co.uk/offices.htm

The Random House Group Limited Reg. No. 954009

A CIP catalogue record for this book
is available from the British Library

ISBN 9781846551734

The Random House Group Limited supports The Forest Stewardship
Council (FSC), the leading international forest certification organisation.
All our titles that are printed on Greenpeace approved FSC certified
paper carry the FSC logo. Our paper procurement policy can be found at
www.rbooks.co.uk/environment

Mixed Sources
Product group from well-managed
forests and other controlled sources
www.fsc.org Cert no. TT-COC-2139
FSC © 1996 Forest Stewardship Council

Printed and bound in Great Britain by
CPI Mackays, Chatham ME5 8TD

Dedicated to Maria Lilja,
whom you may know as Mia Skaili.

"God, what a mess, on the ladder of success
Where you take one step and miss the whole first rung"
—"Bastards of Young," The Replacements

PARENTAL ADVISORY: EXPLICIT LYRICS

In most places where profanity appears in this work, it's basically a matter of authenticity. I tried to leave out the profanity, but sometimes it seemed like betraying the moment a bit. For instance, a scene where punk-rock icon Iggy Pop jumps up on a stack of amplifiers onstage at Roseland in New York and screams, "Nuts to you and your shenanigans!" at people in the VIP balcony strikes a bit of a false chord, wouldn't you agree? When I attempted to edit the line and have him scream, "If you ask me, you're a horse's ass!" it still seemed contrived. Only when I simply used Mr. Pop's actual remark as I recalled it from that evening, "Betcha wish you weren't fat! Jump down here you fat fucks. I dare you to jump!" did the scene come alive the way it inspired me that night. There are other times when the hopefully forgiven, relatively mild profanity seems simply a matter of convenience on my part, and that's sad, isn't it? Mister dirty bird can't even take a minute to find a more mature way of saying something other than cursing a blue streak like an angry motorist or a bitter prison inmate high and insane on homemade prison booze made by cramming a Ziploc baggie with white bread, sugar, ketchup, and fruit-cup remnants from the mess hall, then wrapping the baggie in a washrag and letting it rot and ferment behind the hot-water pipe in his cell. I know, I agree with you. Please know that I'm not proud of my occasional use of even relatively mild profanity in this book.

A more important advisory, though: there's scant mention of some of the best people I met during my relatively short stint of employment. There were people in that office building who loved music and were working there for all the right reasons. I maybe mention two of them. Nice.

Look, I've got some kind of cold today; I'm delirious with fever and I shouldn't be writing a last-minute preface sitting here all twisted up on DayQuil and junk soda like this. It's just that my editor tells me this is my last chance to add anything to this book before it goes off to press, so I'm sitting on the couch thinking, "What would I want to add to this thing if I weren't so high on these delicious, beautifully translucent orange capsules and two liters of yellowy green Diet Mountain Dew?"

Well, there's this to add: I'm honestly grateful beyond measure for this chance that came my way and for the good, bad, and in-between that came of it. It was everything I signed on for and then some. Sure, I've spent a good amount of time wishing the timing could've been better; that I would've had a shot at working in the record business back in the heyday of the major labels. As it worked out, I got in the door just about the time things were falling apart. Then again, there's a little voice inside my head that says maybe that's the most interesting time to show up for something. You know what I mean? Or is that the DayQuil and Dew talking?

D. S. K.
New York, NY

A NOTE ABOUT THE NAMES

The names of people in this book have been changed, with the exception of pop stars, public figures, and three other people. When I asked my friends Nat and Ben if they wanted me to change their names, they asked to be referred to as "Bryce" and "Suck It," respectively; my own girlfriend asked me to change her name to "Cherry Crystal." I did not honor these requests.

ROCK ON

Before We Go to the Office, a Power Ballad That Addresses Following Our Hearts

I'm not a top-notch, grade-A, tanned and successful middle-aged record executive; sadly, you'll realize this shortly. I'm not dictating these pages to a well-scrubbed, starry-eyed, sexy underling on my private jet, interrupted only by nosebleeds that I insist are simply the result of my allergic reaction to a tasteful leather interior and the rigors of daily cabin pressurization. No, I'm basically the guy who made it to the middle and has no problem swiping his ID at the door to let you in for a look around. My biggest qualification here aside from a magnetized laminate that opens a couple of doors is simply this: I've loved music all my life. And you probably have, too, right? Ten bucks says you have. With hearts and brains like hard drives, we all move through this life constantly shuffling through thousands of songs triggered by memories and names, a certain season, or even just the way the light or landscape feels in a certain place. Maybe some of the songs are triggered by a specific small cluttered studio apartment where your ex-girlfriend Kristin seemed to routinely break your personal belongings, then later took to the habit of sleeping with handsome patrons of local restaurants in exchange for cocaine. Or not, I don't know, maybe I'm kind of doing what therapists refer to as "projecting." Anyway, the point is this: our hearts and heads are filled with music, and as years go by we continue to amass a catalog of songs that permanently score some of the biggest moments and memories of our lives; we have that in common, no matter who we are.

I remember my dad teaching me Johnny Cash songs when I was four years old. I would wake up and shave with him before he went off to work, using my toy fake plastic razor and shaving kit. And instead of having to use the empty toy can of fake shaving cream, my dad would give me a little bit of his real shaving cream to use, and man this made me feel like I had arrived. And we would shave and he'd sing "I Walk The Line." I still remember how lucky and amazed I felt that this ninety-foot-tall superhero with his American workingman-tanned forearms and biceps would glance down at me with a grin and take a second to back up and teach me the line.

"I keep a close watch on this heart of mine," he would repeat.

My way of excitedly repaying my dad for these weekday mornings that I would keep in my heart for the rest of my life was to wake the poor man with seizurelike drumming at around seven in the morning on weekends; one toy metal drum, just marching and pounding. First, the length of the hallway in front of my parents' bedroom a couple of times, then the perimeter of the backyard; a pounding and marching that was at once obsessive-compulsive, extremely punctual, and eerily, calmly emphatic — like a new recruit to the Naval drum corps honoring the dead or a tiny drumming version of Christopher Walken. At the age of nine, I bothered him relentlessly for rides to the Toys "R" Us out by the freeway, where I would stare at an Ohio Art brand toy drum set for twenty minutes in total daydream silence, while he patiently waited. Then it was straight home to sit in my room and stare at posters of Kiss and Led Zeppelin in the same wide-eyed quiet trance.

My parents must've lain awake in bed nights, silently considering options like boarding school or exorcism. Because, while my dad dealt with the drum set situation, my mom knew that in the beginning of September she'd have to endure long meetings with me that would lead to deciding which member of Kiss I would be trick-or-treating as, come the end of October. There would be discussions about the details of the actual band's current costumes and whether duplicating them was feasible this year, which makeup would work best, etc. Even though I wanted to be a drummer in real life, I always decided I would be Gene Simmons for Halloween, since his fire-breathing, blood-spewing demon/bassist persona seemed like more fun than drummer Peter Criss's well-behaved domestic cat persona. What was a cat even doing with a demon?

My mom juggled work and everything else she had on her plate with making my demon cape from scratch. She used scissors and stitching to convert ordinary witch wigs into perfect Gene Simmons hair, plus did my makeup exactly the way it was on the cover of the Kiss album *Destroyer*. She never let me go in for spitting fake blood, though. And I was not to play with fire, either. Also, it was made perfectly clear to me that being the Lord of the Wastelands did not give me the right to act like a hooligan; I was to thank neighbors when they gave me candy, and only take one piece unless they invited me to take a bit more. So, each Halloween I essentially became a smaller, oddly well-mannered, polite version of the real Gene Simmons.

There is one sister unit in our little family, who was sixteen when I was ten, which meant one thing: she had the means to buy more records than me. She also had a social life that got her out of the house regularly, which meant I could sneak any new records she had from her bedroom. Elton John's *Goodbye Yellow Brick Road, and then there were three* by Genesis, or *Led Zeppelin IV* — I'd play them in my room on my little record player, and then put them back perfectly so as to leave no clue by the time she got back home. And if you listen to Led Zeppelin at an early enough age, you have to turn it up and picture yourself being in the band and impressing your sister and her cute friends. I would be lying if I didn't admit that, like a lot of the other 18,321,745 grade school kids that the census bureau says were living in the U.S. suburbs in the seventies, my early love of music led to daydreaming that maybe one day I'd be a rock star myself. Maybe you were doing this sort of daydreaming, too. Your resume may even look a lot like my own. A brief review:

- Fourth and fifth grade: Started /lead several lip-synch bands that rehearsed and mimed the bittersweet radio songs of 1976 in Jason Mace's garage. We played brooms and gardening tools, and our set list was basically whatever was on the radio at the moment we turned it on, mostly mid-tempo odes to lost love written by men I always pictured as bearded, very tan, and wearing white slacks and maroon silk shirts with the first four buttons undone. Men who wrote mostly of meeting new lovers while still lamenting a recent divorce. Sometimes the metaphors for lost love were thick and guarded: a horse running free and not returning when its name was called, for instance. Women back then sang a little more openly and less metaphorically of the rigors of love and lust, preferring scenarios of, say, magic men with magic hands, and hoping their mothers could try, try, try to understand that he's a magic man. We lip-synched those songs just as emphatically as the ones from a man's point of view. Jason especially identified with the material back then because his mom and Bob were always arguing about whether or not they had made a big mistake in getting remarried after both having had first marriages that wound up in divorce. During the more emotional parts of songs I'd look over at Jason to make sure he was okay. To lighten things up, I'd give him one of those mid-song nods and knowing grins that you see musicians give each other on stage occasionally.

- Seventh grade: Nearly flawless gig as DJ for Valentine's Day Dance at school, the only real glitch coming when I had to fall back on playing "Stairway to Heaven" three and a half times in a row for reasons I won't go into now, locking peers into roughly twenty-four-minute slow dance. Threats to my welfare were hollered by both boys and girls; even the substitute-teacher chaperone looked pissed by the third time.
- Four-year hiatus after "Stairway" incident: Frankly, I wasn't sure if I'd ever want to work with music again.
- Eleventh Grade: Reevaluated, regrouped, and reemerged at age sixteen with my first band. I played guitar and sang in our power trio. We played at parties. We covered "Repo Man" by Iggy Pop and also played a slightly out-of-tune version of Agent Orange's version of the sixties surf classic

"Wipeout." Our set list took about seventeen minutes to play through, and then we would simply play it over and over again at different tempos.

- After high school: Worked a bookstore job and the requisite record-store job, and later took a job in a wholesale record warehouse near Sacramento. Then I quit the northern-California agricultural-town rat race and drove to Austin, Texas, to finally get serious about starting a career as a singer-songwriter. I returned from Austin to my previous record store job after about a week and a half of what I like to think was a matter of being ahead of my time.

Upon returning, I moved to Seattle, Washington. There I worked a rash of food service jobs and became the drummer in a band of overeducated local girls who had somehow slid into their early thirties as unskilled laborers who loved to drink, with the exception of the bassist, who had a job as an engineer and helped design cranes for NASA. She paid the rehearsal space rent. Aside from the brainy one, our skill sets were a perfect match; I hadn't played drums since I was nine, and these girls had never played guitars in their lives. Together, the four of us found a drunken hobbyist's pleasure in staggering start-and-stop through our dissonant sonic spasms of crude, unformed songs — like stroke victims in some kind of groundbreaking, unorthodox rehabilitation program that involved trying to play electric guitars. We broke up after five rehearsals.

Settling surprisingly comfortably into the hobbies of mild regret, eating poorly, and financial insecurity, I took to hosting a morning radio show at the community radio station on the University of Washington campus. Contrary to popular assumption by my on-air colleagues, I was not a student of the university.

After a few years of embracing life as a pessimist who enjoyed isolation and the seduction of low-grade depression coupled with an awkward lust for drinking too much and then wandering around town until drowsy, I took an uncharacteristic leap of faith out of my comfort zone and moved to New York. And just like clockwork, twenty-nine years after I started sneaking Led Zeppelin records from my sister Trish's bedroom, I got a phone call from Led Zeppelin's record label. They wanted me! Well, they wanted me to take an office job in their marketing department since I had, you know, laid off of the "songwriting" and had wound up working as a copywriter in New York advertising and marketing agencies.

By the time this record label job rolled around, I had gotten honest enough with myself to admit that I was only in three bands in my entire life; one of them was the fourth-grade lip-synch band, the other that short-lived quartet of depressed girls . . . so, one band, really. Maybe the music thing wasn't panning out. Maybe the next best thing would be taking this job and working behind the scenes of rock and roll. I tried to forget those daytime TV ads for a technical institute that I had seen all through my childhood; ads with mustachioed men and plain Midwestern women hunched over mixing boards, staring through a plate-glass control-room window at a recording studio full of musicians who were, for some reason, always wearing outdated, slightly disco-inspired, semiformal attire. The musicians were giving the thumbs-up sign to these ordinary folks to indicate that some knobs and levers had been adjusted to their liking. The ad asked you to "Imagine yourself in an exciting career behind the scenes of rock and roll!" and every time it came on when I was a teenager watching TV after school I used to look at the people in the little glass control booth and think, "Jesus. Look at these poor bastards. Trapped behind the glass and giddy to have even made it that far."

One day on the phone, right around the time I had taken my job behind the scenes of rock and roll, I asked my mom if she thought I would've had a shot at the big time if she and my dad had only encouraged my music a little more when I was younger. Her reply made me feel loved beyond measure, but it also confirmed my worst suspicions: "I dressed you up as the guy from Kiss at Halloween every year. Dad and I helped you get the drums you had been saving for. And then we got you a guitar and some lessons once you were a teenager. Frankly, I don't know what more we could've done."

———————

Come on, it's time to go to the office.

I'm on the subway Tuesday and it's so damn early that I feel the light wave of nausea usually associated with predawn air travel. It's 9:20 AM and the only reason I'm up is because I have to attend my first marketing meeting at ten. After retreating from the nine-to-five New York advertising grind and mainly working freelance from home for the last couple of years, getting to a building in midtown and into a meeting by ten in the morning seems like just another load of crazy talk from folks who've been living well within the staid constraints of tax laws and steady employment.

I get off at Rockefeller Center, walk up Sixth Avenue, and enter the revolving doors at 1290 to catch the elevator going up. Off the elevator and through the twenty-fourth-floor lobby. Aside from the sort of spaceship feel of the lobby up here — with its huge wall of video screens, its unmarked magnetized frosted glass doors, and its hallway lit with recessed floor lighting — the place resembles every advertising or marketing agency I have ever set foot in as a freelancer, except that the ad agencies were a little . . . *less* conservative than this? What? Ah, but look. *There.* In the first office you pass, there's a hint of the rock-and-roll experience that awaits: an electric guitar mounted to the wall with about three hundred laminated backstage passes on lanyards hanging off of the neck. Okay, so maybe there's something vaguely eighties about that particular installation, and also about this particular cream-colored completely unscathed Fender Stratocaster guitar with matching unscathed cream-colored pickguard — as well as the forty-something suburban-dad rocker who looks up at you as you briefly regard the guitar and backstage passes as you walk by. He looks so at home in his otherwise sensibly decorated office that it feels like I've peeked into his dining room at home. The whole vibe is a bit like a "Don't get him started about the time he got to introduce Huey Lewis and the News at Giants Stadium" situation. But still, you can't argue that electric guitars are often used in creating or performing rock-and-roll music, and I think the idea is that backstage passes are reserved for important and exciting people — therefore, I say to you: I am at the beginning of an important and exciting job on the front lines of rock and roll. I keep moving down the hall, down to the conference room in the corner. This is where the magic happens, right? Right. Yes. No matter what, so shut up, because I've been waiting since the day I turned ten — twenty-five years and seven months almost to the day — for something to finally make sense about adults and adulthood, so let me have this. I've been sitting at life's banquet table listening to losing raffle numbers and staring at my handful of tickets for a while now, so throw me the door prize, God.

I meet my assistant outside the conference room. Amy. She addresses a few things that we need to talk about: Do I want paper or electronic phone messages, or both? Do I need my e-mail printed out at the end of each day to be read on the way home? Wednesdays are her busy days because she has to do the TBS reports (I wish I could tell you, but I never found out myself). She can schedule car services for me if I'm working late, or I can also just wait if I don't know how long I'll be working and then get them myself with the vouchers on her desk if she's not around. If I need help or suggestions for my boss's birthday, let her know. Also, she takes notes in this marketing meeting and then e-mails them.

Wait. An assistant?

I spent my twenties barely dodging bullets like nametags and hairnets and now I have an assistant? Okay, fine; I didn't dodge the nametag bullet. Anyway, all you need to know about Amy: a decade younger and somehow a decade smarter with freshly scrubbed New England blonde looks that hint at summers with a large, well-adjusted family spent mostly at a medium-sized lakehouse — an all-American guise to belie the permanent pistol-hot, whip-smart Saturday night grin and a glint in brown eyes that are hiding anything from a joke to a body. You talk with her for two minutes and all you can think is, "Somewhere a twenty-six-year-old man unwittingly awaits severe heartbreak and the kind of drinking where one ends up weeping alone for hours and then dialing."

The fact that I have an assistant is too much to process, really, so I stare at her, overwhelmed and saying nothing, hoping I come off as understated and reserved instead of touched by semi-common mental disabilities. After a brief, barely-oxygenated battle with what feels like the soft, sweet, weighty pull of narcolepsy, I manage to suddenly straighten and swiftly motion with my right arm toward the conference-room door, seeming to suggest that we walk in and find our seats for the meeting. I sit down and take a quick inventory of the room:

- Huge conference table surrounded by super-expensive Germanic-looking chairs on rollers that swivel? Check.
- Big glass windows looking out to neighboring skyscrapers and an heir's view of Central Park? Check.

- A life-size cardboard cutout of, well, a totally anonymous boy band who evidently, years ago, failed to become the next Backstreet Boys or 'N Sync and are now faded blueish-green by the sun and left to tower over us? Uh, check.
- Catered coffee, fruit trays, and tiny muffins cut in half to fuel this rocket ride? Check.

Welcome to the command center for a little starship by the name of SS *Rock and Roll,* sister. Hovering twenty-four stories off the earth's surface. I am awash in imagining that this is the room where my moments of genius will most likely occur. I am drunk on slow-motion visions of saying things and having ideas in here someday that will rescue the record business from peril. And the record business I am envisioning in my mind is not so much a modern-day ivory tower of mogul monsters, but some kind of timeless, broken, and lovable Frankenstein patchwork of people, albums, and songs that changed, inspired, and saved lives at any point along the weird jagged path of American adolescence. That brought a connection to something bigger than our darkened suburban bedrooms through radios hidden under pillows or cheap headphones that somehow made the stretch up to the bed from a cheap little off-brand stereo on the floor next to dirty laundry and unfinished homework. Let's get this meeting going. Let's stoke the fire that kept me and probably everyone in this room alive when we were fourteen and laying in bed, in the middle of the night, in the middle of nowhere, staring at a perfectly white ceiling and facing the fact inside that we were too suburban and polite to ever do the suicide. Knowing we would instead have to take the ride of public schools and years of boredom, longing for some kind of sex, even though we couldn't even figure out how to have it, and never thought we would actually get it. Let's go. Somebody say something. Fuck it, I'll break the ice; unthinkable usually, but then again, right now I'm connected to a force in the universe larger than I will ever be or have ever been.

"Is that a, um, blueberry one?"

Jesus, I'm an idiot. Not what I had in mind to open with.

"This is chocolate chip."

"Oh, okay, chocolate chip. Okay."

"It's good. What's wrong with chocolate chip?"

"Nothing. No, I'm not saying . . ."

"Are you turning your nose up at it?"

Holy Christ, is she serious? She looks kind of tough, this woman. But in her defense, she's wearing a hippy sundress that looks like it could be made out of hemp or recycled paper towels; she's an angry, aggressive tempest in clothing made by kind, passive people in Oregon. She seems mad, like she was mad before this exchange, I mean — like she's been mad for years about something. Maybe it's an act; she's probably another perfectly respectable mid-thirties Caucasian-female passive-aggressive creative type from, say, Venice, California, who has realized the only way she's survived for a decade here is to be perceived as tough.

I try to size up the stern look on her face, but when I do I think it looks like I'm staring her down. I swear to God I was just saying it nervously and nicely and just being the new guy making small talk. I really don't care about the stupid muffin. Why would I be turning my nose up at it? I want to tell her that I've spent plenty of afternoons in the last three years standing in my tiny kitchen eating everything from bouillon cubes to pieces of leftover burrito and stale holiday candy, all within minutes of one another, all while staring out the window at this beautiful, ageless, and indifferent city, drinking from a carton of milk, wondering when my next freelance gig would come. Christ, there were plenty of points in the illustrious Bush Jr. economy when I would've gladly risked the misdemeanor of stuffing a chocolate chip muffin down the front of my pants in a Greenwich Village deli and running until I found a place to catch my breath and eat it.

"So, what, you're new, I guess."

"Yeah. Hey, I didn't mean to . . ."

"We haven't really met. I'm Beckah."

(long pause) "Sorry, I didn't catch . . . is it Rebecca?"

"Beckah. I didn't catch your name because you didn't say it."

I pause again, staring at her and trying to think of a mnemonic device that will prevent me from suffering a future scornful stare when I call her Beth or Chaka. I think of something like, "Chocolate chip muffin for a woman named Rebecca, then just take away the 'Re' and you've got Beckah." I'm certain I'll forever know her as "Chocolate Chip" or "Muffin."

"Anyway, I just thought it was blueberry because . . ."

"Yes, I know. You pointed that out," she says with the kind of stressed thin smile angry people force onto their faces on occasions that require at least a visible attempt at good cheer.

Whatever. . . . I just kind of raise my eyebrows and refocus.

Ms. Chocolate Chip is the in-house music-video producer, and frankly I don't care what she thinks of me. Sure, it's not very strategic, this rare bout of self-confidence I've chosen to indulge. But, I look across the table and Vallerie, my boss, is smiling, so I am relieved. What can I tell you about Vallerie? She's a senior vice president here, my direct boss — the person who hired me on — and that makes it even a little more awkward that I basically live in fear that I'll wind up in a meeting absent-mindedly writing her name over and over on my binder or notepad like a seventh grader with a crush on a teacher a few years before he learns to deaden unexplained feelings with heavy metal, canned beer, and petty crime. At one point she was a model living in London and was on the cover of an album that was in every one of my friends' older brother's record collections — and I probably started noticing her right around then. She's fifteen years older than me, look, quit freaking out — Jesus! Yes, she's beautiful; we're all beautiful, okay? Shut up. Drop it. She's older than me. She's my boss. I was just trying to describe her. I'm not saying I have a crush on her. God. Fucking act like an adult.

The meeting starts and the first order of business is talking a bit about the progress of the new Fat Joe album. I write the first meeting note on the fancy notepads they gave me with my name and the company logo on them: "Who is/are Fat Joe?"

The Fat Joe album is coming along, evidently, and then talk turns to Fat Joe's work strike. Something about some rumor of not continuing on the CD until the label buys him a thirty-thousand-dollar fur coat that he's had his eye on.

"What?" I start laughing, but turn it into a cough super fast, when I realize that this is apparently nothing to laugh at. Duly noted. It's so weird, though, especially since I'm starting to gather that this guy is some sort of gangster hip-hop rapper guy? Maybe it's a joke everyone is making? Maybe it's a joke that Fat Joe made? I have no idea at the moment, but I look around the table and they seem to be sort of serious. And then someone starts to say something else about it and is quickly interrupted so that the meeting can move along.

I sit there trying to make a face that that says, "Listen, I agree, it is not a laughing matter." I keep a straight face — a feat I'm starting to realize is the secret to succeeding in business — and the meeting passes in what shifts between a slow, deadening grind of numbers and dates and a fast amnesiac flash of upcoming highlights. And somehow after an hour of this, the rapper wanting the coat already no longer seems funny or ridiculous to me. Whatever, I'm the guy who wants a fat salary, expense account, perks, and stock options to write and produce the rapper's advertising campaign between the hours of ten-thirty and six, so what am I laughing about? Me and this dude are in the same racket, basically.

The product managers in today's meeting consist of a couple of twenty-something guys who got the lucky break after working their asses off for a year or five as assistants, and a handful of suburban folks who look like your average neighbor in a pleasant leafy suburb, save for a requisite shock of bright red hair dye, or — in the case of one woman from radio promotions — a dicey middle-aged venture into the land of leather pants worn without a trace of irony. There's one woman, thirty-something and slightly more metropolitan than the others, whom I would say resides in the file of: married smart, risked little, gained a lot, prefers to think of herself as "chic" and prefers to spend weekends in their house in the country instead of the downtown loft they bought. The thing that draws your eye to her is how she clearly concerns herself with being stylish and smart in every regard, except for the fact that she's very attached to a particular denim jacket that I would have to guess, in a conservative estimate, went out of style approximately two decades ago. She seems to have a studied, natural way of flaunting it in a variety of settings, the way an Ancient Pueblo tribesman might flaunt a colorful blanket he was awarded as an elder chief or tribal councilman. She hangs it on her chair, she tosses it over her arm, she drapes it over her shoulders — which she scrunches up toward her ears, indicating to all that she's evidently chilly. In her office, she leaves it hanging on the back of her chair, proud embroidery facing out to passersby. I recognize the jacket from when I walked by what must be her office on my way in this morning. I can only assume that her one exception to a wardrobe that otherwise refrains from dating itself to the Reagan Administration must have something to do with the status that comes with having the phrase WORLD TOUR embroidered above the right breast and the word CREW atop the left, and the same stitched words repeated on the back of the jacket (in case you didn't catch it when she was coming at you) along with the band's name and the year of the tour. I size up her mid-thirties petite frame, manicured hands, and well-moisturized, unweathered face and decide there's no way she actually got her start as a thirteen-year-old roadie for Genesis, humping the band's gear in and out of stadiums around the globe in 1981 during the *Abacab* World Tour.

Topping off the assembled marketing folks this morning, we've also got one very handsome metro-sexual gentleman who should be making side money modeling in cologne advertisements if he isn't already. He's sitting to the left of me; and he's a man who seems too suave and smart to get very tangled up in any of this — but he is, because he speaks up and starts off a domino effect, and one by one, all of the product managers take a turn at weighing in with a report of what's going on with the artists they're in charge of working with.

"Okay, Junior Senior; really good phones; adds are huge, doing paid dates — like, mostly DJ stuff at clubs. I'll talk to radio about the second single. Pantene is a yes from Linda if they're still looking, she might be a little outside the demographic, though, so we'll see. I'll know if Brandy is a yes today, but it depends when they want to deliver and what the Jewel situation is. I still need approvals for hotel, air, and that girl for nails and facials. Spins are up for Junior, too, forgot to mention that. If Chris moves to PD at Z100 then, well, we'll see what happens there, but . . . right now the first single's crossing to everything, Modern AC to AC and even a few AAA, researching great across the board."

It's funny how fast forty-five minutes passes when you have no idea what anyone is saying whatsoever. I pretend I'm familiar with the words they're throwing around; I listen intently to what they're saying, nodding with a pretty steady frequency that I start to worry could appear too steady, and almost syndromic. I find myself essentially acting not unlike a dog that's simply tilting his head, excited by whatever phonetically pleasing sounds seem to cut through the clatter of the unintelligible.

As we finish and file out, little fragments of their marketing monologues are still swirling in my head and forming a surreal little lyric to start the day with:

Why don't you think Jewel would do Pantene Pro-V?
If we book the Super Bowl is it all lip-synch then
    meet-and-greet
or are they letting people sing?
Still waiting to hear about Kid Rock for *Letterman*
but we would have to fly him private
to make it in time.
Spins are up on everything for me
And we worked out the Nappy end caps thing
Phones on the single will help
We're also going to street team it
We need to wait and see
About in-stores
for Kill Hannah.

I'M PAID TO WRITE LOVE NOTES
TO PHIL COLLINS

Leaning back in my office chair with my feet up on my desk, as I believe one is supposed to be posed at moments like this, I stare up at the ceiling pensively — toying with a couple of pens from a brand-new, fresh box. My posturing is informed by old movies like *Big* and *Wall Street* and a scene I recall from that TV show *thirtysomething*. I probably look like I'm thinking pretty hard, but I'm basically still trying to decipher the code that the product managers were speaking during the morning meeting. It is, however, time for me to actually get started on my first big assignment.

Before we get to the first assignment at the new, intense, high-profile rock-and-roll job, let me first admit that there is a delusion I have apparently quietly indulged since, say, age thirty, and it's this: that I am still as cool as I was when I was seventeen. Inside the heart and head, a sort of suspended animation. A never-quite-acknowledged freezing of time. Unmonitored, this is how the tragedy of uncles who "still get high" happens. And now having taken a full-time job working on the marketing and advertising of bands — somehow this delusion is raging in a very bad way. In the days leading up to this job, I've spent a lot of time laying on my couch, listening to my iPod and daydreaming about how I am basically going to be paid to be some sort of intense über rock-and-roll person who is marketing loud, fierce developing bands that are not yet registering on the radar of the so-called normal, run-of-the-mill adults in the mainstream. Those were great, powerful, and beautiful moments of delusion, mostly because I had not yet sat down and faced this first big assignment: to write an inspirational and congratulatory ad campaign that celebrates twenty-five years of heartwarming love songs from Phil Collins.

I've been told that one of the ever-changing copresidents of the company wants to make sure I understand that my ad campaign is going to be targeted largely to females forty to fifty-plus years of age, so I need to be writing in that voice. The first thing I do is pace around the temporary office they've got me in, wondering how the hell I'm going to do this. I start trying to write some headlines that I think forty- to fifty-something-year-old women can relate to. For some reason they all sound like those Hallmark greeting cards that aren't really for any occasion in particular. Like, they're usually filed under a section called "Just because" or "Friend."

- Remember the first time you heard that special voice?
- Here's to the voice that taught us about love.
- Who was *really* your first love?

In a quiet panic, I cut those headlines and I jump to adjectives like *biggest-selling, chart-conquering, platinum-smash,* and then I land on the word *hero.* Yes! He's a hero! Okay, maybe not a hero, I think to myself. But maybe there's a word that's not really hero and not quite as big as God, but something kind of less grandiose and somewhere in-between. I decide I've got to dig deep. This is my first assignment and I'm convinced this is one of those quasi high-profile New York

LIMERICK COUNTY LIBRARY
005719921

jobs where if you don't really nail your first assignment, they fire you. I've got to get into this guy's head. Who is he? What makes him tick? Think, man!

Okay, stop. You're freaking out. Pull it together and let's consider this for a second:

What do we already know about him?

We know that he admits he *can't hurry love.*

He has also said that he *can't stop love.*

He is also someone who — even with all of what's going on in the world today — thinks it's not *too late for love.*

And overall he's got a clear understanding that love is a loving feeling you get when you fall in love *against all the odds.* Plus, he has enough humility to admit that his love doesn't stop even after — and this is kind of interesting — the other person has stopped loving him. In this new song I'm listening to, he's literally saying that he *can't stop loving you.*

If you were to look at the Time Warner building from the outside at this moment, you would see a perfect grid of glass and steel divided off into square offices, and in each of those offices somebody sitting still and confident at a desk or table. Except for one little square in the grid where a little man was pacing back and forth and looking up at the ceiling and silently saying, "Fuck. Fuck, fuck, fuck." And asking nobody in sight silent, mimed questions like, "What am I doing here? What am I going to do now? What was I thinking?"

Well, apparently here's what I'm going to do now: I'm going to go start selling *myself* on twenty-five years of heartwarming love songs from Phil Collins. It feels like when I was in my twenties and made the mistake of finally joining one of those records clubs where you get to choose twelve albums free if you buy two more at regular club prices. You know that disheartening moment where you've chosen the only remotely cool albums for your twelve free ones, and you still have, like, six more to choose? That moment where you're sitting there alone convincing yourself that you really *do* want the Crash Test Dummies album without the hit and, say, *The Essential Leonard Bernstein*?

"Okay, look," I say to myself, "the fact is this: Phil Collins is a guy who has lasted twenty-five years in a business that eats people alive. You think he has a day job? You think he's in an office trying to figure out how to make his boss happy and keep his job? He does whatever the hell he wants. I mean, if I'm so into what's cool and what's *not* your average adult, well, this guy doesn't have to wake up at nine to be at work. I mean, listen, say what you will but Phil Collins is doing whatever he wants to do."

By day two of this assignment, the inside of my head is doing things like this: "Hey, who am I to have any opinion about the songs or music this guy is writing? How many songs have I written? None, that's how many."

Day three:

"I mean, who's to say I even know what Phil Collins's songs are about. I mean . . . 'She's an easy lover, she'll get a hold on you, believe it?' Come on, man. . . ."

"*She* could be anything . . . it could be a metaphor for the establishment for all I know."

"*SHE'S AN EASY LOVER?* I mean, he's basically saying the government is screwing us. So, anarchy is the only solution, is basically what he's saying."

My boss walks in to see how things are going. Hair, eyes, smile, whatever, not noticing, not noticing, not nervous, not nervous. I'm concentrating so hard on not being nervous, that it probably looks like I'm thinking. She stands at the front of my desk, as if she's not sure about interrupting me, but then: "So, have you had any time to work on the Phil Collins thing?"

Any time? *Jesus,* sister; I've been here for three fricking days losing my mind on this thing; like Sheen's character in *Apocalypse Now* when he's locked in that hotel room.

"Hi," I manage.

"You can stop wherever you're at with it. I just talked to Phil and his manager on the phone and they don't want to make a big deal out of the ad. They were actually really cool about it and basically said that at end of the day it's, you know, pop music and they don't want the label to make a big deal out of it."

"Wow. Yeah, exactly. I was kind of in the same . . . yeah, that's so cool of him to say that. He seems pretty cool. That's totally . . . I totally agree with him. That's cool."

She continues, "So, they'd like the ad to just be a picture of Phil and the number 'twenty-five.' Not even the word *twenty-five.* Brilliant, right?"

Going through my head: What? A picture of the guy's face with a number next to it? Where's the writing in that? There's no craft in that. You don't need me here. Why are you paying me?

"Well, you know, yeah, if you look at it from a certain angle it is a very nice, simple, elegant ad. Sometimes that's kind of a good way to go, you know?"

When It Began, or
The Twenty-Nine-Year-Old White Guy
from Orange County, California,
Tells You About Soul Music

Right, so there's a question that comes to mind. It's a question that I've been asked by family members and friends entirely too often already: how did I even get this job? I guess the only answer is that it probably all began with this commercial I did when I was freelancing.

I was twenty-nine years old, hung over, and standing outside the office of the late George Jackson, then president of Motown Records. Like the winner of some kind of cruel and indifferent essay contest, or the victim of an especially inventive hazing, I was there to show Mr. Jackson — and evidently also rapper Ice-T — what I felt the fortieth anniversary of Motown Records meant to folks. How the hell did I get tapped to make a television commercial commemorating the history of Motown? There was nobody more suburban white-bread than me in this city, this *building,* let alone walking around on Motown's floor in said building. It didn't help that I was so sleep deprived from the long nights put in during this strange little random trial by fire that I felt like I was going to cry at the stray notes of a Boyz II Men ballad coming from a small portable stereo somewhere down the hall. Standing there in front of Mr. Jackson's door and hoping to God that I did this right, I started feeling convinced that God was nothing more than a bored man on a cloud with a plain old-fashioned cruel streak who didn't mind toying with people like me for kicks. I had been in New York only a year at this point; just the typical delusional inductee to the city, staying out late every night and getting maybe three hours of sleep before reporting to the entry-level work I had turned up at a high-pressure C-list PR firm; work that basically involved writing press releases and magazine ads for a decreasingly popular brand of blank audiotape. The owner of the PR firm was an openly and unapologetically bitter man who blew cigarette smoke in my face as he shook his head and marked up my drafts with red felt pens, all the while his index finger absentmindedly fishing around in the ever-present little bottle of pills prescribed to restrain the fits of stress-related ticks in his head, neck, and right shoulder. The honeymoon, I like to call it.

Anyway, I got this Motown gig because of Dave, whom I had met by chance as soon as I landed in New York, who worked on staff at Atlantic Records, it turned out. He called and asked if I would be interested in talking with someone at Motown about some freelance work. Motown had asked him first, but for obvious reasons he couldn't work for another record company on Atlantic's dime, so he called me and asked if I wanted the work. Dave's generosity confused the hell out of me. I didn't question it and would soon learn that it would be exactly this type of kindness and generosity that would save my ass in this city. I came to New York thinking it was a small and cramped violent island infested with drug-addled dreamers, desperate comedians, charming small-time street thieves, and dubious banker types — but that has not been my experience, to put it mildly. I gratefully accepted Dave's kind gesture of keep-

ing me in mind for this break, and since there was no con-
flict of interest with my nine-to-five job at the chain-smoking
bitter man's PR firm, I said yes, that I'd love to do a little freelance and create a TV commercial for Motown's fortieth anniversary. Never mind that I had never created a TV commercial
before, let alone a TV commercial that would attempt to sum
up four decades of soul music in sixty seconds. Oh, and kind
of tie it to a thematic summation of what I thought it meant
to be black in America. *Our struggle,* if you will. Anyway, how
hard could it be to write and produce a television commercial,
right? Here is what I say to the children who are our future:
never underestimate how denial and a good old-fashioned
mild learning disability can team up to come off as unwaver-
ing self-confidence.

When I initially met with the people at Motown, I got
scared realizing what I was getting myself into. I started accidentally soft-selling myself for the project a little, and I think
it came off as confidence. They would say something like, "You
know, this is about more than music. This is a soundtrack to
lives. And we want to convey that in the commercial. George
sees it being this spot that reminds the viewer of all the things
that happened in the country in these forty years." And I was
freaking out inside, so I would just sort of stare pensively out
the window, trying like hell to think of something — *anything* — to say to them. And then calmly, almost catatonic from
fear, I would say something like, "Well . . . you know . . ." —
long pause, debating whether or not I should just tell them the
real situation and how they're going to need someone who has
made a TV commercial before — "It's . . ." — Come clean, you
are *nothing* — " . . . American history, yeah, but . . . it's also the
American . . . *Dream* we're talking about here." Oooh, that one

even impressed me a little somehow. The man who was so into the creative process he couldn't even look them in the eye was onto something; it's true, though, what Berry Gordy Jr. did starting a label in Detroit on eight hundred bucks borrowed from family, a risk and passion that goes on to make history, that's the soul of the American Dream.

Full disclosure on how I was almost accidentally able to summon self-confidence during this period: I was still getting used to wearing prescription glasses for the first time in my life, and they were really working some magic. Aside from being able to read more than a paragraph of text without falling asleep almost instantly, I was taken aback by how smart they made me feel in moments like this. You say something like that without glasses on and people might be like, "You're not really paying attention. You need to stop staring out the window daydreaming and focus on what we're telling you." But when you do it with glasses on, it's more like, "Oooh, look at him staring out the window, then down at his shoes, then out the window again. Shoes, window, shoes, window . . . what's he *thinking*? What makes him *tick*? What's he about to tell us?"

I went away from those initial meetings confident in my understanding of what they wanted to convey, and how I could see it through creatively. The only thing I wasn't sure of was how to go about doing stuff like getting pictures.

I spent the next few days writing a script all about — you know, what . . . what it means to *feel* soul music. And I took this direction from George to have these huge numbers hitting the screen before we land on the number "40." Numbers that tell us how many riots ("3") our people have seen. How many of our men marched in D.C. ("1,000,000"), etc. I spent another week using the Internet while I was at work in order to research how to buy stock footage of things like historical civil-rights demonstrations, footage from the Apollo space program, footage from the Apollo theater, how to contact Martin Luther King's estate to get permission to use still photos of him. I was allowed to hang out in the vaults at Motown all by myself, albeit with a guard at the door during my visit and an archivist logging numbers, codes, times, and dates for every photo I touched or wanted to take for production. And everything in the photo vault went back to day one. All the way back to snapshots from Berry Gordy Jr.'s personal collection stowed in envelopes, old boxes from Detroit film labs, flat file drawers stuffed with sleeves of negatives. Outtakes from some of the most famous photo sessions in the history of American music! One envelope I found was filled with an original round of prints from the shoot for Marvin Gaye's album *What's Going On*. He was in his backyard — you'd never know it from the final front cover because it's cropped so tightly, but I'm sitting here thumbing though this stack of faded color prints from that day and the legendary Marvin Gaye is, for just a moment, a man just like anyone of us, standing in a suburban backyard that is littered with kids' toys. And just out of the frame of what ended up a legendary Motown album cover is a swing set and slide. He towers above it in a full-length black leather jacket. Just over the fence is another modest house. Between takes, he just looks like someone you could've been living next to then, but connected to something huge. It's easy to look at the pictures and imagine some sort of eerie moment where you poke your head over the fence to say hello like a good neighbor and realize the guy next door is tapped into something in the universe so huge, so much bigger than the both of you, and you just back away slowly.

I picked up another envelope and opened it up. Just an ordinary old business-size envelope, the kind you buy at a drugstore, softened and wrinkled, white but faded, and the adhesive on the flap is brittle and yellowed. In aged pencil somebody has written the year 1975 on the corner of it. I reached inside and pulled out an old Kodak snapshot of a young Jack Nicholson, smoking a joint, sitting at the soundboard with Stevie Wonder during a recording session and laughing; I just stood there with my index finger on the edge of glossy fading proof of an America where handsome, hilarious, merrily deranged silver-screen outlaws dropped in at recording studios to listen to what a blind funk genius was laying down onto reels of fat, wide, warm, two-inch analog tape thirty years before the digital age. Stood there thinking about the world outside and wondering if I was born too late.

Boxes and envelopes yielded print after print and sometimes 35 mm or medium-format negatives. The Supremes in front of the house that was the Motown office and studio that Mr. Gordy named Hitsville U.S.A. Right there, 2648 Grand Boulevard, where he started it all with an eight-hundred-dollar loan from his family. Another faded and yellowed snapshot: the Four Tops driving a big American steel convertible in Detroit, huge humble grins, suits and shades and hearts, a moment that hits you so hard you're standing there realizing you've never *really* tried. Look at those guys! They will play what they play because it's in their blood and they will play it whether or not the world showers them with millions. Has nothing to do with whether or not they make the money, score the award, grab a shoe endorsement and a video game tie-in, or get a reality show made about them. They look at the camera like they are going to do what they do and if you want to catch the ride, great, and if you don't, what's that got to do with what they're doing? They sure as hell aren't gonna switch up their sound based on focus group research or chasing a bigger audience or check. Here are pictures from a time when singing soul meant you had some.

I grabbed all of them to use in the commercial. The archivist logged everything that I took. I left and got on the subway back to my day job, where there were some ads about blank tape to be written. I called up Ben, the video editor at this place where I freelanced for a week when I had just moved here to New York. I explained how I had all of these photos and a script and footage and had gotten all of the requisite legal clearances, but that I had no idea how to make it all into an actual TV commercial. I told him how I was doing this thing on the sly because I had the Man looking over my shoulder at my day job. So we started building the commercial over at Ben's editing studio working nights. Maybe from seven to two or so in the morning on any given evening, and I figured that when it was time to show it to the people at Motown, I would sneak out and do it on my lunch hour.

Getting back to the moment at hand, that's exactly where I am: on my lunch hour, standing nervous and sleep-deprived outside the forty-eighth-floor corner office with Mr. Jackson's assistant, waiting for the green light to go in. In a few seconds I will have to walk in and say hello and try to do a hopefully-not-clammy handshake with him — the handshake? Do you do the handshake when you're in this position? Should I try to throw it down kind of soul style in my little Banana Republic nine-to-five junior PR writer ensemble? The door opens and I walk in, keeping pace to the staccato rhythm and groove my brain is stabbing at me with each step:

Oh.

No.

Suit.

Lawyer?

Wait!

Ice-T!

Is here?

Small hands.

No way.

Just shake his hand.

Normally!

Mr. Jackson's big-hearted, robust introduction is filled with the kind of love and generosity that I am misguided and naïve enough to think must be found in the halls of every major record label on the planet. A big man, maybe 250 pounds of him, and his handshake and love for what he is doing here almost throws my medium frame across the room. I've managed to navigate a straight path to the big leather sofas in the corner of his office ready to show this thing. Okey dokey, Mr. Jackson and . . . Mr. Ice? Oh, good question. Would you say Mr. T? No, don't say that. That's the guy from that old show on television.

After all of the late nights editing and the days spent lost in the archive, after listening to the advance copy of the fortieth anniversary CD a million times, I am strangely confident in what Ben and I have created, but a burst of self-confidence is almost always a disaster warning for me. I put the tape into George's VCR, and he starts tweaking an enormous console of preamps, patch bays, and equalizers from the leather chair he's sitting in — it's a scene that looks like a 250-pound black man is commandeering the bridge of the starship *Enterprise*.

The slate on the commercial counts down backward from ten like movies in school did, and on the last beep, the commercial starts in. The opening riff to "Superstition" pumped through speakers that look like they belong in the space program. Totally lethal speakers that I've never seen in the consumer sector, and on the screen forty years flash before our eyes. JFK, Marvin Gaye, Apollo rising from the launch pad, a still young and innocent Michael Jackson with his brothers clowning around on the streets of Tokyo during the first Jackson Five tour, Los Angeles in flames more than once — 1965, a routine traffic stop sets L.A. on fire for six days in Watts; 1992, L.A. is on fire again after the Rodney King verdict comes in, an edit that makes you wonder if anything has changed — and Stevie Wonder singing, "Very superstitious . . . writing on the wall," cut back to Martin Luther King saying he has a dream over the top of Stevie Wonder's riff. Goddamn, I've never noticed how much MLK looks as innocent as a child when he says it, you don't see an agenda as much as a man just doing the right thing in the eyes of his mother. Cut to a shot of that motel in Memphis, the one that the gunman had in his aim when he pulled the trigger that morning in April of 1968; cut to a black-and-white photograph of Berry Gordy Jr. standing on the porch at Hitsville U.S.A, a young man about to go farther than even his wildest dreams for this thing; cut to the Supremes on Ed Sullivan's stage; cut to the Beatles hanging out with Berry Gordy Jr., and his baby daughter. This is the same spirit that made colonies, that went west, that went to the moon and back, this man starting out against the odds with a small loan in his pocket, he winds up making history.

Damn, why hasn't this commercial hit me like this until now? I watched it played down a hundred times in the editing

studio. Maybe I drank way too much last night after we finished what we figured was our last editing session, and now
I'm too hung over to be watching it and, Jesus, I think I'm going to cry or something. What if the lights come on and Ice-T
sees me standing here crying? He will kill me. Have you heard
this guy's songs? Jesus, he probably actually has a song about
killing guys that look like they're about to cry over their own
commercial.

The spot finishes and George's assistant is about to turn
on the lights when George says not to. Thank God. Maybe he
doesn't want to be seen getting ready to cry? But then George
says the reason we're leaving the lights off is because we're going to watch it again. Oh, shit. This means they've found a
mistake or something. Why did I take this on? At the end of
the second time, the lights come back on. These two men are
still facing away from me, and they stay seated, not saying a
word. I'm standing an arm's length away and slightly behind
them and it's quiet. Way too quiet. George Jackson, without
looking, out of nowhere pulls back his huge arm and punches
me hard in the shoulder. And since his hand is about the size
of my entire head and neck region, I am off balance and tilting, now falling, slow-motion up against the wall. Shit. I got
it wrong. My slow motion fall up against the wall continues,
and while it's all happening, I'm thinking: *I swear, I'm on your
side, brother.* Strangely, I still have a nervous polite smile on
my face. I settle up against the wall; it's still quiet. And then he
starts laughing. Through his huge booming laugh and with a
smile in his voice, George Jackson says, "Dan Kennedy! Goddamn!"

And Ice-T says, "That's right, you know what I'm sayin'?
What you did right there, you showed that it's history. It's mu-

sic, yeah, but it's a part of America, see. That's what makes it so . . . so moving."

I readjust my body so I'm not falling against the wall anymore. Kind of make it look like I was done with what I hoped came off as a casual and confident leaning, as opposed to being a medium-frame white guy who was knocked off balance and startled.

"That's why the man gets paid. Right there. That's why," George says. I think at best I managed to quietly mumble something like, "Hey . . ." then.

A week or two later I'm in George's office to talk about doing an ad campaign for the Marvin Gaye remastered CD that Motown is releasing in a few months. About ten minutes into this visit, Stevie Wonder walks into the room. My twenty-nine-year-old brain tries to process the string of events:

1. Hung over again.
2. On my lunch hour, need to get back soon.
3. I am shaking Stevie Wonder's hand.

Mr. Wonder reaches into his pocket and pulls out a small DAT tape, telling George that he recorded this song at home last night and that George absolutely needs to hear it, that he feels like it's one of the best songs he's ever written. Holy God, I am going to hear a song that Stevie Wonder wrote less than twenty-four hours ago. A song that he's standing right here saying he thinks is one of the best things he's written.

"I'm tellin' you . . . George, you gotta hear this. Put this in and turn it up." This from Stevie Wonder, now standing about fourteen inches to my left.

How is any of this happening? In my head, I reel and stagger, trying to figure out what any of this means. Does this mean my life is the type of thing where I spend my lunch hour sitting around with the man who wrote "Superstition" and "Higher Ground," shooting the shit, listening to demo songs, having a laugh? Have I been admitted to some club that I don't even realize I'm part of yet?

"Hang on, let me get finished with Kennedy about this TV stuff and get him on his way here. Then you and I, we'll sit down and we'll listen to it."

———————

Duly noted.

FURTHER PERSONAL NOTES ON SOUL MUSIC

Most insightful thing a white guy has ever said to me about soul music:

"I never could've written anything as good as that Marvin Gaye song, because after I wrote down the word *brother* once, I'd get stuck. I'd be sitting there going, 'Let's see . . . what else can I say here? I just used the word *brother* so I can't use that again.'"
— My friend Loren Victory, 1998

I'M TOO EMOTIONALLY UNAVAILABLE TO WRITE A SOUL SONG

Me and my girl
seem to be doing fine.
She's been pretty busy with things
I've been pretty busy with things as well.
Anyhow, no complaints, really.
Me and my girl
will probably take a trip this summer.
We've both been wanting
to do something
in order to get out of the city.
Yeah, so . . . anyway.
Chorus: It's been nice here this summer.
Hasn't been as humid as it usually is. [repeat 3x]
So . . .
How are you and Kate doing?
(solo)

Changed His Name
So I Don't Get Sued

I'm basking in the afterglow of having the Phil Collins head-line situation behind me when Amy pops in to remind me that there's a sales and marketing meeting that I should attend. I tell her I wish I was still young like she is. She assures me that I'm vital and have most likely outfoxed the terrifying wave of good sense that can make zombies out of men by their late thirties. She looks me in the eyes and tells me that I don't need to worry that my adolescent dreams have given way to office hours, lattes, conference rooms, an odd and passive unrequited crush on a woman fifteen years older than me, and sitting in my office thinking about how much I envy the assistant that is ten years younger than me. At least that's what I infer from her when she says, "It's the sales and marketing meeting, and it'll be mostly be sales, actually — just to let you know."

Walking into the room, there's a carryover of some folks who were in the meeting where the muffin situation occurred. The flock of product managers, Vallerie, and an aged Robert Wagner type and several of his brethren, two of whom are rocking sort of eighties-suave Alberto-VO5-dry-look-hairstyle-and-affordable-blazer getups. They lean way back in their chairs most of the time, almost tipping backward it seems, only occasionally sitting up to write a release date in a handsome leather day planner with their expensive, ornate ballpoint pens. Not sure what department they're from.

At the head of the table is the guy who used to be another record executive's publicist back in the day. He's the general manager, but for a while there he was a copresident, I think. Or maybe that's what he is now. At any rate, his name is Bill, but don't worry, Bill, I will change your name if I write more about you so that you don't get all in a knot and have one of your tantrums where you scream at people. So you don't yell at grown female executives at the top of a twenty-five-year career and make them cry, as we've all heard the reports of. I will change your name so that you remain anonymous here, and also so you don't sue me since you make a seven-figure salary for doing whatever the hell it is you do here and you have a lot more money than I do. So don't worry, Dick.

A collection of thoughts that run through my mind when I first see the way Dick tends to treat people who aren't the pop stars that he is so unapologetically over-the-top sweetly accommodating of:

- My, you're a delusional power-drunk little angry hornet in very expensive clothing, aren't you?
- Someday I will stab you in the leg with an ordinary pair of office scissors like a modern-day Boo Radley, finally fed up for good with the way you treat others, Sir.

Today, Dick is demanding that everyone in this room do anything it takes to make the newly signed band on the hand-outs in front of us into huge stars.

"We are going to make this happen" — pause for dramatic effect that will hopefully offset his small, boyish, and frankly strangely lovable, voice. "We will not stop until these guys happen in the U.S. and even then we're still not going to stop, because Europe will be next. They're going to be huge stars, and we have the rough cut of their first video in here today, we'll watch it, and I think you'll see what I'm talking about."

He keeps addressing the room in a slightly perturbed effeminate voice and demanding that these guys become stars. It somehow tugs at heartstrings I didn't even know I have, the way he keeps talking about how we need to make this happen. The sales guys have a can-do attitude on their faces, but you get the impression they're savvy enough to make a can-do face even when they don't think they can do something. Younger product managers sit attentively, shifting in their seats uncomfortably the more Dick says that failure is not an option; older VPs seem to be looking down a lot, or at one another for some kind of quiet confirmation, but mostly looking down at whatever notes or PDA gadget is in front of them.

It all feels so fake, this kind of demanded enthusiasm; like we're building forts out of sofa cushions and making machine-gun and grenade sounds with our mouths to go with the pantomime of our imaginary war zone, except instead of innocent kids playing for fun we're all thirty to fifty years old and the fort is in some high-tech, huge conference room at the top floor of this building in New York City, so we're supposed to act like it's all for real, and really important. I do actually *feel* important, which is kind of cool.

Dick looks over at Suave Older Robert Wagner Character and SORWC quickly turns off the Evil Underground Lair light switch, and the lights perform their overly choreographed shutting down, stuttering a sublime flash sequence that leads toward the screen at the end of the room while smaller key lights simply fade down in perfect timing as the music comes

up. In the conference room on the twenty-sixth floor, that's
what's simply referred to as turning off the lights.

Okay, look up at the huge screen at the end of the conference room. A ten-years-too-late Eddie Vedder look-alike stealing Jim Morrison's moves. And a bassist and guitarist who
move in a way that seems to be saying, "Yes, you learned lead
singer moves in our local college's night class on how to be
a rock star, but never forget that while you were doing that,
we were studying how to posture ourselves properly as well,
and we have just as important a role as you. See, we indicate
that we're passionate about the guitar playing in the band."
There's dancing, pouting, and these bored and angry mood
swings that seem to say, "We're angry. No, we're sexy. No,
we're bored. Wait, we're angry again. Hey, now we're longing!
We are, in fact, feeling everything you could possibly want us
to feel — But no matter what we're feeling, we're rocking."

I have a hunch that everyone here knows that this band's
biggest problem is that they're not so much authentic as they're
trying to indicate to you that they are authentic. We sit there
smiling politely and watching.

The video ends and in much in the same way as the newly
signed band mimics being rock stars, those of us sitting around
the conference table mimic being moved and inspired by the
young men mimicking being authentic rock stars. There's got
to be some kind of scientific name for the chain of mimicry
going on here.

Someone politely and quickly taps the big touch-screen
remote control console in the center of the table, another person on the periphery hits the lights and they fade back up slowly
and methodically, revealing Dick in a sort of Dr. Evil pause at
the head of the long conference table. He looks at everyone

lining the table and conference room walls and says, "They . . . are . . . going . . . to be stars. They . . . are . . . going" — hold it for a beat. Hold it, wait for it, and — "to be huge." The basis for this thinking, as Vallerie was kind enough to clue me in on in the hallway later, is:

1. They have a huge manager and are a huge priority with him and so they'll be a huge priority with us.
2. Lead singer is the brother of a rock star.
3. Lead singer knows how to "move."

I feel like we're all looking for the quality of genius around here — in ourselves as much as in new bands. But something about what it takes to survive in a corporate setting has me feeling further away from being a genius than I've ever been. But, you know, obviously I never say that. I mean, come on, you won't get anywhere admitting things like that.

So You Wanna Be a Chart-Topping Rock-and-Roll Star Embraced by Major-Label Marketing Executives and Corporate Radio, Well Listen Now to What I Say.

1. Lead singer type: You need to have "moves." Moves should be odd combination of sexual advances and a temper tantrum, punctuated with moments of apparent hypoglycemia. Best-case scenario, you have long hair that is worked into moves. If it helps, use some mnemonic devices or prompts to help remember the order and choreography of the aforementioned "moves." (See below.)

   a. "Where's your wallet?" (Grabs own ass with right hand.)
   b. "Is your crotch okay?" (Pushes pelvis out, seeming to look down at it out of the corner of his eye as his head and hair fall to the side a bit.)
   c. "Show me where the camera is." (Points toward lens in video or television performance. In live performance, change prompt to "Show me where the exit signs are"; this should elicit a pointing motion to horizon out past audience.)
   d. "Can you see where we're sailing to, Captain?" (Puts one leg up on the monitor at edge of stage and looks out.)
   e. "Shame on you." (Hangs head down with arms at side. Use this prompt during long guitar solos that leave lead singer type without much to do.)

2. Lead guitarist: You should look bored, as well as skilled in Web-site development, including back-end architecture and server-side technology. You should also appear to be courting an iron deficiency in the blood. It should be

unclear as to whether the iron deficiency is from long hours developing e-commerce and mobile blogging application or touring with band.

3. Bassists: You should be prone to being emphatic with instrument, regardless of how simple bass line to song is. I've said this before and I'll say it again, bass players: I've only ever met one woman who understands that you aren't playing the guitar solo in the middle eight bars of the song. And the only reason she understood the difference between the lead guitarist and bass guitarist is because she was a brilliant bassist. So, bottom line, when the guitarist is blazing away, go ahead and take a step forward with your bass and sell it with an intense rock face, humping motion, etc.

4. Drummer: You should be even cuter than the lead singer if you want this band to be huge. It should be almost statistically improbable that you wound up doing anything in a band that doesn't involve your face being prominently displayed within savvy proximity to the front row.

Hi, Do You Guys Carry Picture Frames, Little Mahogany Boxes Covered in Alligator Skin, Little Pen Holder Things Made of Leather, That Kind of Thing?

There are little moments when God gives you a sign; gifts, I like to call them. They are these sort of conspiratorial winks from the universe that let you know what you're doing is getting out into the world; that you're affecting something in your time here on earth. One of these gifts has just been sent to me here in my little temporary office — my first piece of produced work; a paid advertisement on the cover of Billboard Magazine with a huge picture of Phil Collins's face and the number "25" next to it. As I stare at the paid-advertisement-disguised-as-magazine-cover with confused pride and confidence, there's a small team of workmen painting a bigger office down the hall that I'm set to move into on Monday. Which brings this next little strait to navigate: I never really thought about it until today, but the fact is, I don't have anything to move into my new larger office. Aren't you supposed to when you land a job like this? At this point in my life, the only nine-to-fives I've held briefly rewarded me with a cubicle and, in one instance, a supply closet that was converted into an office. I didn't take the time to decorate these spaces.

But everyone here has tons of stuff in their offices — pictures, platinum albums, furniture, and just . . . stuff. Stuff, I don't know, like a Zen tray thing filled with sand and some little polished stones or something — whatever you buy when you're thirty- or forty-something and you've been on track since you graduated college at twenty-two. "They'll be done with audio and video and painting in there today, so if you want to move your stuff in over the weekend, you can," this from Vallerie as she passes by my door on a routine flyby.

I call my girlfriend, Maria, at her office and ask her what Vallerie means by this and what your average thirty-five-year-old normal man would be moving into his office, if he were accustomed to having an office.

"I wouldn't worry about it. She probably just meant you could start working in there now that they're done painting and stuff."

I immediately disregard her level-headed input, deciding that *clearly* she just doesn't get it; she's not a winner if she's not second-guessing everything, she's not going for the gold, or something. Actually, screw gold; she's not going for the *platinum* in this life if she isn't thinking about this sort of thing. Okay, so maybe ever since the muffin incident at my first marketing meeting, I've been nurturing a mildly degenerative paranoia. This thin film of corporate workplace insecurity is a charming personality attribute, to be sure. An attribute found mostly in middle-aged, overdressed, status-insecure folks with sketchy self-esteem who are hoping to climb the proverbial ladder of success, and small-town crystal methamphetamine freaks convinced that little men with walkie-talkies live in the walls and phone. What we share — the middle-aged go-getters and the psychotic meth addicts — is a constantly aggravated, malnourished, and cagey sixth sense that tells us *everything* means *something* and that people are *noticing* even when we *think* they're not. And the way we see it, people like my girlfriend *simply don't understand.* I decide that this weekend I will make up for lost time and acquire all of the things that normal successful people move into their offices with. I will catch up with them that quickly, these normal on-track people. I will fit in if it kills me, and be a bigger, more well-adjusted version of what I am. Hell, I'll be bigger and more well-adjusted than them! I look in magazines for photo spreads of successful people's offices. I watch that movie called *The Kid Stays in the Picture,* that biography of Robert Evans, and I stare at everything in the background of his office. I think that's where I picked up the cue that successful people have a lot of framed photos in their office. Which is basically why I'm here in the Home and Office section of Saks Fifth Avenue.

"Excuse me, how much is this one here?"

"The tortoise shell with silver inlay? That's a wonderful choice. Beautiful."

"It sure is. It's . . . a . . . nice . . . picture frame."

"Let me check for you."

It feels completely indefensible, being here amongst over-priced decorative items and buying into all of this. I worry about bumping into somebody I know. I move hyperdiscreetly the back way through aisles, like a paranoid high school math teacher visiting a strip club too near to the small town where he lives and works. This place is right down the street from the office and seems to have a total understanding of how to appeal to people plagued with a deep need to be seen as successful. At least I'm dressed for the part, so I probably don't stand out much, I mean, half of the stuff I'm wearing came from here. I should back up. I'm, well, dressing in gray slacks, black sweaters, and five-hundred-dollar shoes these days. It's impossible not to notice that all of the guys in charge kind of dress like a slightly more hip J. Peterman catalog — and like a lucky poor kid adopted by the rich in a bad sitcom script, I've decided I'll do anything to fit in, to not get kicked out of this club. I would also like to point out that my sensible navy blue designer windbreaker jacket costs $675, and the salesman at Barney's tells me it's great because I can wear it inside at the office when it gets a little cold from the air conditioning.

Nice.

That's very manly, isn't it? But it all somehow makes sense to me in this kind of nine-to-five mild codeine high I get from strolling around with a head full of recycled air that's been filtered through twenty-three floors of stylish nylon executive carpet and assorted veneers and Formica; it's a high that feels like a thin barrier between me and the real world outside. Out there life is still happening and those poor bastards are dealing with silly little everyday problems like love and death.

Christ, I've got a monkey on my back. An office job is like an indefinite five-day-a-week Vicodin and wine binge; it changes you. Speaking of changes, I will only say this about my new hair situation: the highlights were supposed to look much more rock and roll than this. The most awkward thing about the highlights that I let the hairdresser talk me into is that older Puerto Rican women *love* them. Apparently highlights are a big thing in their community. They'll come right up to me in a Starbucks or on the subway, stare up at my head and coo, "Ooooh, I low your highlight!" while I stand there in awkward silence. I usually act like I didn't hear them, but if they keep staring up at my head, I say "Thank you" very quietly.

So, the first picture frame to have caught my eye here at

Saks, the one the salesman is checking on, is this huge-ass desktop tortoise-shell number about the size of a manhole cover or storm window. This frame says, "I have a very impressive picture frame and therefore have certainly not, as you might expect, spent the majority of my so-called post-college years self-employed and jamming envelopes of cash in a hole up under my bookshelf, hoping to somehow outfox adulthood with an intoxicating tonic of binge spending and low-stakes tax fraud."

The salesman's posture belies the malady of the middle class; an almost obsessive-compulsive attention to body language, a studied focus on hand gestures and policing of the voice's inflection that hints at a seminar on how to "carry" one's self—the kind of disciplined spasms and ticks a sort of discount finishing school for the class-insecure might instill. It draws the portrait of a man furiously trying to politely distract others from a long personal history of fair-to-middling winnings in life's cruelly random lotteries of class, genetics, and fortune. Okay, clearly, I'm projecting. Anyway, he's finally back with the price.

"Three seventy-five."

Holy Christ! Three hundred and seventy-five dollars for a picture frame? How much if you take the cocaine and diamonds out of the hollow part in the back of it? Do. Not. Look. Surprised. You are supposed to be very normal and successful, and this is probably how much normal and successful people pay for picture frames. "Oh, good. Yeah, three seventy-five, okay, good . . . I'll, uh, I'll take it."

But you need a lot of these things. So I buy others, too. A tasteful little teak number with lighter tropical wood inlays. One that looks a little bit like a cross between a seashell and a coffin lid, one that looks like . . . bumpy . . . leather? I split and head across the street to Banana Republic where the frames are much cheaper, it turns out. And I buy even more there, mostly simple and pedestrian stainless-steel frames that will benefit from hanging out next to the Saks frames. The next stop is Takashimya back on Fifth Avenue. The store that has apparently cornered the New York market for small boxes covered in alligator skin, large and stately leather-bound journals, small bowls made of bone or antler or something, and a handful of other important stuff like little trays made out of wood, leather, or stone. I get a nice assortment of all of the abovementioned accessories. What the hell, I even tell the saleswoman to throw in a long, skinny three-compartment tray made out of some kind of dark tropical wood, teak, maybe, a real nice little number that I might use to casually store bulletin-board pins in or maybe some change from my pocket. I decide against a four-inch silver ball that comes with a little suede bag to put it in, and consider briefly maybe getting the $275 rustic set of two pewter cups (pen holders?). I have spent well over fifteen hundred dollars, and aside from the frames, I couldn't tell you what you're supposed to do with any of this stuff. It's time to go. My plan, so I don't get caught and ridiculed, is to just drop it off at the office over the weekend.

I have, maybe, twenty frames at this point. I figure if the idea is that I actually went to college and I've been out of college for, say, at least twelve years at this point and, say, had offices for the last ten years, then that's about two frames for every year of my steadily employed, level-headed adulthood. Never mind that I don't even have twenty friends and loved ones, so I start going through the process of figuring out what the hell I'm going to put in these frames. At home, I dig deep through closets and boxes. There are some snapshots of people I haven't heard from in ten or fifteen years. I will frame them for my office because it's all I got. So I haven't heard from them in a decade, they fit the part. Look at Jeff! It's before he grew his big hair and his long sideburns and beard and moved to Berkeley. He looks all clean-cut in this photo. He's wearing a wet suit and holding a big crab, and it looks like maybe I know a clean-cut scuba diver, but really we were super hung over in San Francisco and had rented some wet suits and boogie boards at the beach. And there was this huge dead crab at the edge of the water, and Jeff picked it up to huck at something, but before he did I got a quick snapshot. It looks like he caught it while diving in his fancy wet suit and is inspecting it for eggs or something. Just like a marine biologist would.

I've got only sixteen frames left. And I still have the huge tortoise-shell frame. I get a little sad and awkward when my girlfriend tells me that this beast is usually used for something like a couple's fiftieth anniversary. Yeah? Well, guess what, Maria; I'm out four hundred and twenty bucks with tax and I refuse to wait forty-five more years until I can put a picture of us in here.

It's Sunday, and I've asked Maria to come along with me to the office and give me some input on how I'm setting things up.

"Why are you putting leather coasters on your desk?" She asks.

"So people can, you know, put their drink down when they come into my office. A Diet Coke or whatever."

She stares at me.

"Would you like something cold to drink?" I ask.

"No . . . thank . . . you," she replies slowly while watching me figure out where to display my wooden box with alligator skin on the lid.

I know this stuff is all a big dumb lie. I'm starting to think half of what everyone my age does is a lie. But I want to try for once in my life. I want everything to work out; I want to fit in here, and to be regarded as important and intelligent. I want everyone to think I'm a normal and successful man like the others, accustomed to going to his office, then home to his loved ones, and then back to his office again, loved ones, office, loved ones, and so on, and so on.

Anthems for a Seventeen-Year-Old Girl, or "Duran, Duran, and . . . You Are?"

Monday morning here in my new tastefully decorated normal adult-size office, and at the moment there's a pop star standing with a big grin in front of my door. Okay, so maybe Simon LeBon was a pop star twenty-three years ago, if you want to get all technical. Okay, fine, so he's not standing in front of my door because he needs to talk to me so much as he's standing there having his snapshot taken with the guy who works in the office next to mine. Which, yes, if you want to be a stickler for details, obviously means his being all smiles is just a guess on my part, as he and this other guy's backs are turned to me, trapping me in my office. I'm sitting there thinking that if any of my teenage efforts at being a drummer or guitarist in a world-famous band would've come to fruition, and let's say I would've been the drummer in Duran Duran — this is exactly the view of Simon LeBon I would've had nightly for my entire time in the spotlight. So for a minute, in a weird little way, it's like I'm living the dream. After the snapshot everyone continues along their way, then a couple of bosses walk by and poke their heads into my office on their way to the Duran Duran meeting.

"Hey, quit working so hard and come down to the conference room and say hello."

To which, in fairness to myself, I have the corporate savvy *not* to reply, "Oh, I'm just checking out my friend Ben's Web site that he built for his band and trying to figure out if there's a guest-book thing you can sign on here." Instead, I remember that success in a corporate environment means always appearing busy, confident, and outgoing. I remember how my friend Josh recently busted me — told me that I could really no longer fall back on the shy loser shtick that got me through my twenties when it seems I'm doing fine for myself in my thirties. And you know that sort of gay little voice in your head that goes, "Yeah . . . he's right! I'm going to go down to the conference room and introduce myself to Duran Duran in front of my bosses, because this 'quiet guy isolated in his office and not taking any risks' thing is going to stop!" If you don't have that voice in your head, just try to remember the voice that convinced you that you should try dancing drunk at a wedding or office party. I hear that voice and I get up out of my chair with my goony, doggone-it-I'm-going-to-choose-life confidence.

I walk down to the conference room in my sensible gray sweater, black slacks, and black leather Prada shoes. Everybody is in the conference room already; Ms. Chocolate Chip is looking right at me clearly wondering if I've got the balls to walk through the door, so I ignore her as I step in. Suburban Classic Rock Guy is there. Aging Robert Wagner Character From Sales is there. A smattering of vice presidents is in attendance. A gaggle of lesser-paid-and-ironically-more-qualified-than-everyone-in-the-room assistants and product managers stand around looking genuinely happy and effortlessly cooler than everyone in middle and upper management. I've got that burning sensation on the back of my neck that comes from making a late entrance to a work thing like this. And apparently it's the late entrance that comes with the misunderstanding that maybe I'm the guy the band is waiting to meet? I ask because I'm deeply confused when, for no reason that I can discern, Simon LeBon takes the initiative to get up from his seat at the conference table and extend his hand to me, which makes some small gland somewhere inside of me shoot into a spasm resulting in a burning, red-hot shot of adrenaline speeding straight into my bloodstream, which triggers a warning in my head to keep it together and not say something stupid. And so when we shake hands, I just stick to the first very basic thing that pops into my head and say, "I'm Dan Kennedy," evidently a little too loudly in a way that sounds surprisingly way too confident. I start to panic in my head when I hear the voice boom from my upper chest area, and see three other guys from the band turning toward me when they hear it. I do the only thing you can do, which apparently is to keep repeating a slight variation of what you just said with each new handshake until you think of a way out of this. And so the guitarist puts his hand out and I grab it and repeat, "Dan. Dan Kennedy," in a tone that my little internal adrenal meth lab has now turned in to a weird mix of loud and happy. But it's a loud and happy that's mixed with a slightly boisterous, mildly inappropriate confidence; like that of an armed forces recruiter enjoying tempting small-town youth with discipline problems into a reservist program that yields a modest payout to barely cover textbooks and a couple semesters of tuition at the local college after enduring fifty or sixty weekends of vaguely homoerotic torture in a boot camp. I have to quickly think of a way to make sure there is no misunderstanding, especially with my boss in the room. That I'm not delusional enough to think I'm upper management or something and that Duran Duran shouldn't think so either. So for the bassist, when I reach out and grab his hand, I switch it up and say, "Big fan. Bigfan." *Jesus, somebody mace me. Have the compassion to put me down and get me out of this.*

The "big fan" line doesn't help reverse any of the situation at hand, since now they're kind of looking at me like, "Well, good thing this guy's a big fan. Wow, we're already off to a great start here." And I'm thinking, "No, I mean, I'm just a fan to you. That's all I am, just another, everyday, ordinary, one of millions of ordinary fans. Not the booming voice and whatever that implies in a conference room at a record label where you're talking about a possible deal." And then there's a fourth guy, and he's not reaching his hand out, so I make the effort since my adrenal glands have now apparently tightened into a *series* of twitches that tell my brain to shove my arm out in front of me. And in a slight variation of my last greeting, I tell him I'm a big fan of *his.* "Heybigfan. Of you."

Somebody. Anyone. Slam 60 ccs of Klonopin and Valium into my shoulder with the hard punch of a thick needle like they do to inpatient escapees or discount inbred quarter horses.

So, I'm locked into staring at this guy's face trying to recognize him. *Wait, which one is he? Okay, think about the "Rio" video from '82 where they're all on the yacht that's racing across the ocean. Okay, visualize it . . . the guy on the bow was Simon. I recognize the other two guys. They were sort of standing in the middle section of the yacht. Who is this guy, though? Was he maybe in the boat's galley fixing lunch or something and you couldn't see him? I mean, it's not like I was into them enough to recognize them twenty years later. Although, I did just holler over and over again that I am a big fan. Okay, this is not the time to figure it out, let go of the guy's hand, it's been twenty seconds or something.* Soon chairs are shuffled, everyone who isn't upper level brass is asked to leave. The meeting is getting under way, and I recede and fade, walking backward out of the room with a pleasant and vacant look frozen on my face, convinced that the line between today's anxiety attack and tomorrow's stroke or unemployed cross-country spree of petty theft committed in a blackout is thinner than ever now that I'm working in an office full time. On my way down the hall, a product manager walks by having just exited the same meeting.

"I can't believe I got to meet Simon LeBon. I got a picture with him. Did you see that," he asks.

"Yeah. Hey, who was the guy with short black hair sitting to the left?"

"I don't know, I think he's their manager. Or maybe their road manager, I'm not sure."

All I can think is: *Well, whoever he is, he knows he's got a big fan.*

Rock Opera Trilogy:
I. The Donnas Sing Songs About Sex in Cars
II. Be Cool, Stay in School, and Leave the Fully Automatic Assault Weapons at Home
III. Jewel Is a Human Being, for Your Information

How can anyone not like this band, the Donnas? Or maybe more accurately: how can one thirty-five-year-old straight white man receding into the melancholy of middle age not like a band of cute girls, ten years younger than he is, playing a solid stadium-rock song about having sex in a car with a faceless male protagonist? Deadly combination, if you ask me. The only combo that might be slightly more powerful would be the same band of girls playing power ballads about sexual loopholes that don't technically constitute cheating on one's wife or high-energy anthems that detail ways to avoid getting gouged on taxes this year. Anyway, decent band; paid major dues in the first portion of their career on a small independent label; and they've now taken the jump to a major label, having signed with Atlantic.

They've got the requisite indy guitars-up-front sound with a mild hint of indie label post-punk vibe, which will be briskly and freshly scrubbed off of them quicker than you can say "Budweiser wants to pay you to be in a commercial." They're good looking, they play guitar songs in 4/4 time that are loud and have this kind of tongue-in-cheek take on lyrics and maybe a certain nod to seventies stadium rock with the requisite twenty-something hipster wink of irony. I wonder, though, is there anything sincere about hipster irony? Can you even imagine Joey Ramone ever standing on a stage and thinking, "Man, this is hilarious — I'm being totally ironic; my hair is hanging over my face, I'm super tall, and I'm singing about some place called Rock and Roll High School? Get it? Me? In High School?" Say what you will about what became of punk or seventies stadium rock, but my hat is off to the lack of irony. I applaud the fact that Kiss never came off stage saying, "How classic was that? I was all, 'Alright, New York, do you people want to rock and roll all night?' and then I was all, 'I can't hear you!' and they yelled even louder! I think they thought I was serious!"

Anyway, here in the studio up on the twenty-eighth floor with the Donnas, we're waiting for a couple of other people I work with to show up. The band's product manager arrives with some big wig from radio promotions or New Media or something. We're going to be recording thirty-second public service announcements about how kids shouldn't bring guns to school — which kind of seems like a given, but whatever. These little announcements will feature the band saying something to the extent of, "Hi, we're the Donnas, if you hear about something or see something out of the ordinary" — namely, your peers toting assault rifles — *and we're guessing that would strike you as out of the ordinary* — "let a teacher or your principal know. Check out our new album, *Spend the Night!* at a record store near you!" or something along those lines, and the world will be a better place. They're really cool about it; their attitude is pretty much, "If it stops one kid from

doing something horrible, then it's worth it" type of thing.
And I guess the label's stance is more like, "If one person, plus
five and a half million other people, hear this public service
announcement, possibly prevent a tragedy, but more important, head to retail to buy your album, then it's worth it. . . ."

The in-house studio is basically two little rooms hidden
behind a sort of James Bond blue vault door, and the door
just looks like a part of the long, high-tech, space-age hallway here on floor twenty-eight until you realize there's a little
handle tucked away that turns part of the wall into a door. It's
crammed with racks of preamps, boards, monitors, and about
seventy-five other high-tech flashing, blinking, slim, and impressive things that I have no idea how the engineer operates.
How much did this place cost? is my first thought. The studio is
used mostly for recording things that it seems you could just
record on your laptop — like these public service announcements we're doing today, or what they call "drops." Drops are
when you get an artist to say, "Hi, this is ARTIST NAME and
when I'm in CITY, the only radio station I listen to is NAME
OF STATION THAT LABEL HAS PERSUADED TO PLAY RECORD
REGULARLY."

I'm standing in the first room of the studio, next to a leather
designer couch that exceeds my station in life and a mixing
console manned by today's engineer. I hand each Donna the
little scripts I wrote; there are a few different versions of each
one. I'm a little nervous about the fact that they're so attractive, although — and I'm sure unveiling the following ruse
isn't breaking news, but: no star looks quite as gorgeous or
handsome in real life as the five or six-figure photographer's
version of what they look like. The first time I saw Jewel at
the office it took me ten minutes to recognize her even with

four huge posters of her new album cover on the wall of the hallway we were both walking down. I was shuffling down the hall that day thinking, "Who's this attractive blonde woman walking toward me? Think. She . . . looks . . . very . . . familiar, but I can't quite . . . Connie, maybe? From accounts payable? Yes! That's her. That's who does the expense checks! Wait . . . is it?" And I kind of nodded hello as we passed in the hall and as soon as I was ten yards past my brain made a positive ID and I was thinking, "Wait just a minute. That was Jewel. But with pores. And a normal, human-sized waist." Enough time, money, lighting, film, and Photoshop airbrushing, and you can make America fall in love with the oddly tiny, slightly hooked little toe on my left foot. Yep, give me the standard budget of one to three hundred grand for a shoot with the right photographer, stylist, and art director, and I'll show you an unsightly little toe that gets e-mailed marriage proposals and has legions of gushing fans bringing that photo to plastic surgeons and hair stylists, saying, "I want to look like this." Still, the Donnas are very attractive. I've walked into the studio from the control room to hand them their scripts, and am hoping I've written them in a fashion that gets across the sober tone of discouraging teens from bringing fully automatic firearms to school, while at the same time still managing to capture the playful, rockin' tone of the band and their song, "Take Me to the Back Seat." That's the song that will be playing in the background while members of the bands are telling the teens not to bring guns to school.

"So, do you like your job?" one of them asks me.

"Yeah . . . you know. Whatever. I guess it's pretty cool as far as jobs go. Man. Pretty, you know, chill."

When I hear it come out of my mouth, it sounds like a tape

of an undercover cop trying to convince downtown perps that he's not a square. Or one of those cheesy modern dads trying to get his daughters to think he's cool so they'll admit to drinking beer on the weekends and then he can lecture them and insist that if they're going to drink, they do it at home.

"You know . . . I kinda just do whatever I need to do and nobody really asks me any questions. Yesterday I took a two-and-a-half hour lunch with a friend. Whatever. What are they gonna say? You know what I mean?"

Just then, the product manager and the vice president or whatever from radio come in from the control room. The product manager is one of the guys that spend a solid four-year stint working his ass off as an assistant before getting the break; one of those guys who started from the ground up to get his job and has wanted it, has tasted it, longer than I've even been in the building.

"Hey, you guys! You look great! Did you have a good flight?" This, from the product manager.

"Yeah, it was good. Kind of tired, we played in Boston last night and today after we do MTV stuff, we have radio stuff, a dinner, and then we'll play at Irving Plaza tonight."

"Oh, wow! Okay, well this shouldn't take long, we should have you out of here pretty quick. I see you've already met Dan."

And that's when it happened. To this day I can't remember which one started it. I think it was the bassist.

"Yeah we met. He was telling us how he takes two-and-a-half-hour lunches with his friend and nobody says anything."

Then the other girls in the band start laughing and chiming in.

"Yeah, he's all, 'What are they gonna say?'" This from the one who sings the songs about slutting it up in people's sedans!

I give them a look while biting my lip, bulging my eyes a little bit, and barely shaking my head "no" in hopes of discreetly stopping this. But there's no way to get them to turn back. Maybe it looks like I'm freaking out and that's why they're saying even more things. I feel like Schwarzenegger before California made him governor, when he's in that movie where the kindergarten class is getting out of control and he can't stop it. *Kindergarten Cop,* I think it's called. He's like a big lion being harassed by a pack of hyenas or something. Another one of them speaks up.

"Yeah, we asked him if he likes his job and he was like, 'I guess . . . if you gotta have a job' or something like that."

What? Drop it! Jesus, you guys sing about tempting motorists with sexual favors or whatever the hell you're singing about and you're telling on me?

I stand there with a terrified polite little smile frozen on my face avoiding eye contact with the product manager and vice president, waiting for that moment when the three of us would start laughing. After five or six seconds of silence, it becomes apparent that this isn't one of those moments.

"We should get started on these," I say to no one in particular.

I walk back into the little control room on the other side of the glass so we can get started.

After a handful of takes, one serious, one sweet, one rocking, it's time to leave. They take off their headphones and we all file out of the studio; I close the door and it fades back into the wall. We say good-bye; they keep asking me if it was good enough. *Yes, God, it was good enough. Just go. You've done enough.* They walk down the south hall back to fancy elevators that will gently set them back down on the street twenty-six stories below so they can be on their way to their hotel before playing for a venue packed with adoring fans. I take a different elevator. An elevator that takes a much shorter trip two floors down. Time to get back into my office, check my e-mail, surf the Internet, and, well, heal.

FREE LYRICS FOR ANY ALL-GIRL ROCK BAND TRYING TO WIN OVER THE MIDDLE-AGED WHITE SUBURBAN MALE DEMOGRAPHIC

I think that's muscle, not fat.
I think you're hair's still rad.
You and your friends still seem like rockers.
It turns me on, the way you tuck your short-sleeve Polo
into your pleated khaki Dockers.

Hey, baby, did you hear?
Big changes in the tax laws this year.
You can write off almost all of your travel
Doesn't matter if it's business or personal.
What? [sexy moan] Oh, yeah!

[Chorus]
Hello, Sir, we wanna do it to you after the show.
Hello, mister, we could do it and your wife would never know.
We wanna have two Amstel Lights
and party till eleven on a Tuesday night, yeah!

I think your four-door rocks.
I love those sandals with those socks.
I swear to God you turn me on.
It gets me hot when you brag about
Underreporting your gross annual income.
[solo, repeat chorus, to END]

For Those About to Rock in Vallerie's Office, We Politely Salute You

I'm staring at the calming, soothing colors of the calendar on my computer screen when suddenly Amy interrupts my post-Donnas healing process.

"We're all heading down to Vallerie's office to hear this guy that they just signed."

Act like you don't hear her.

Out of the corner of my eye, I can see her still standing in my doorway.

Ignore her. She answers your phone. She can't boss you around. She's so nice, though. I want to be young again like her. Jesus, easy, Sport.

"Vallerie's office in ten minutes if you want to hear this new guy."

"Oh, yeah. Good. Just checking . . . things on my computer. The calendar there. Good. Looks good."

There is something entirely surreal and uncomfortable about being crammed into an office with your coworkers and bosses while a newly signed star-to-be sits in an ergonomically correct office chair with an acoustic guitar and emotionally croons about heartbreak and sexual mishaps; almost always about the general rigors of young hard-living lovers plagued with emotional problems and bound for quasicrippling emotional disaster designed to bring a tear to your eye, it seems.

I mean, I'm not saying I even find them particularly moving. I'm just saying . . . we're all being shoved into an office together listening to songs that are supposed to make you cry . . . and we're at work. So I'm concerned that, you know, worst-case scenario, somebody gets choked up in there; that would be a little awkward. And the musicians who do this, they always look completely comfortable in their skin, oddly enough. Totally fine doing this. Most people would feel pretty damn awkward even talking too much about a health insurance claim while sitting in somebody's office, but these guys seem to be able to sing about relationship difficulties, struggles with addiction, sexual problems, emotional inadequacies, you name it! They seem to be saying, "Want to hear an intimate performance of my song that talks about my inconsistent weight, surprisingly positive sperm analysis, divorce, and subsequent pill addiction? No problem, which office do you want me to play it in?" My hat is off to them. I can't even talk to my boss about my weekend plans without stuttering and blinking my eyes seven thousand times.

I don't want to go to this. If Amy's supposed to be my assistant, why do I have to do everything she tells me to?

I'm going to start stabbing myself in the arms and chest with a Bic Paper Mate pen as soon as the new genius starts to sing, how's that for a little number about emotional difficulty?

I shuffle into Vallerie's office with some other stragglers and there he is. Really thin, kind of shaggy hair and a small chin beard. You've seen this guy in every university district of every city you've ever been to or lived in. He's the guy who's muscular and gangly, bright-eyed if it weren't for being a little stoned, and he thinks he's cute and charming when he says something wittier than the other street poets and beautiful losers when you walk by. Something like, "Hey, support your favorite starving musician, man. . . . Got a spare million bucks or a spare record deal, maybe?" I usually smile and maybe sometimes give the clever self-referential singer-songwriter types a spare dollar and walk on. Well, apparently someone gave this one a record deal. He's got a friend, too. A bit more meat on his bones and he's the one who plays the guitar while the other one sings. I can't help picturing him sneaking money out of the guitar case on the street when the singer's not looking; he's seriously, like, fifteen pounds heavier and the other dude looks like a lean lost dog. They sit there quietly waiting for us all to file in. What if a fax comes in on the machine they're going to be playing next to?

Everyone is here. The smattering of VPs, Rob/Dick, Vallerie, Amy, Chocolate Chip, the product managers, Aging Suburban Classic Rock Guy, Aged Robert Wagner Character From Sales. Dick says something in an introduction to the lot of us about how brilliant these two are. Which, really, is simply his way of saying that he has heard from someone above him that somebody here thinks these two are brilliant. Wouldn't that be such a sweet introduction? I bet even these guys getting ready to play for us would start cracking up if Dick went, "Welcome to Vallerie's office, everyone. I've never heard of this young man with the guitar, or the guy sitting next to him who apparently doesn't play an instrument, but trust me when I say it's probably a good sign that I've never heard of them. Anyway, I have been told by my boss to tell you and your bosses that they're brilliant, and I basically do whatever the bosses say. That's my own problem to deal with. Anyway, let's hope Vallerie doesn't get a fax while they're playing — hit it, guys."

If he had the heart and guts and sense of humor to say something like that I would follow him to the end of the earth, seriously. If we collectively had that kind of heart and guts as a company, we would have the coolest bands on the planet wanting to sign with us.

The guitarist starts to play as the other guy sings while smacking his legs like a focused and caffeinated psychic teen runaway keeping time to a beat that only he can hear, and only when he closes his eyes.

Slim starts in with his singing: "Yeah, she's gone again. Whiskey and cigarettes. The front door slams, heartbreak and nothing left, but she's . . ."

It gets heavier from there. Sentiment about feelings, emotions about pain, and frankly, the guy's doing an amazing job of describing these, well, just sad feelings that . . . you know? What I mean? Jesus, try not to look at the others in the room. Don't listen to what he's singing. Don't think about it, just try to look like the guys who run entire divisions of this company; calm, cool, a reserved and polite tap of the foot or bob of the head. Just do that.

I can almost, I mean, with his gentle strumming and singing about this stuff that screws all of us up, I can almost see every executive in this room as they were when we were all . . . innocent . . . children. I'm just saying, you have to be a human being about it, you know? You can't stand here and say this isn't moving. It feels like when you see a Mother's Day commercial that makes you cry because you're tired or a little hung over. Man, how do things get so messed up between two people? What the hell goes wrong with love? Why does some love last and some just blows up so fast? Or worse, blows up in your face after so long, when you never thought the end would come. Why can't we figure love out! Nobody knows. God, how do we settle for some of the messes we all get into, these things that should've ended years ago by the time they finally fall apart. I . . . I love my girlfriend so much. We're really good for each other. We have a lot of love and a lot of laughs together. We're kind. Kind to each other, because that's what . . . what love is. That's what hearts do. But getting close to somebody, that's how we all got hurt at one point or another. Everyone in this room. It's scary, you know? Opening your . . . your *heart* to somebody. I wonder if I'm ever going to be a dad. More love near us, more life around us. Or would it be a drag somehow? It could be a total drag. Everyone says that having kids changes everything, but what they don't tell you is that so does sitting in a studio apartment alone in your forties. I'm so afraid of marriage, and all that. It just freaks me out for some reason. As if it could ruin everything we have and we'd be stuck like that. Christ, I'm probably screwing up every good thing in my life because of fear. I feel like I've been so lucky to have ever been in love and have loving feelings that seem to love like a lover who . . . *Holy Christ, you're listening! Snap out of it! The song's got you in its grip!*

Look around the office and get your mind off it! Now, dammit! Look at anything! Stare at the Stone Temple Pilots platinum plaque like you've never really noticed it! "Hmmm. Interesting plaque. I love that band. 'Interstate Love Song' was a great song," I seem to be saying when I look at it, tilting my head a little to indicate that I'm really appreciating it. I keep looking around the room, so these guys can't make me have feelings. *Hey, I like the way Vallerie has her plant right there*

so it kind of covers up all her phone lines and computer cables.
Good thinking. That's smart. Hey, nice picture frames, she's re-
ally got some good ones. I try to think about the first time I
heard the Pixies and that feeling of walking around college
towns aimless in life, but happy to at least finally feel connected to something. I think of anything I can to get out of
this sad love song's grip — like ineffective names for hardcore
death metal bands. I distract myself by building this list in
my head:

Ineffective Names for a Hardcore Death Metal Band

> Light Tropical Storm
> The Peppermint Twists
> The Trolleymen
> Fine Living
> Gene Doubleday and the Fall River Players
> Hoopla!
> West Burlington Death Metal Combo
> The Ginger Snaps
> Scrimshaw

Actually, that last one kind of works.

The song ends. No way, they're getting ready to start another slow one. Jesus, please, we get it: Love is hard, and there
are a lot of difficult emotions in life. Let's wrap it up, I need to
get some fresh air and some sweet food to shove the feelings
back down.

The guitarist is taking a few minutes to tune up again. And
the singer/leg smacker guy actually has these little raps between numbers. And those are what really make me like him,
because they sound exactly like the little raps I say in my head

every morning on the subway to work trying to rationalize
every little compromise I've made in life. He says something
like, "I just want to say that we are not here to become what we
have never been. We're here to do what we do — but, I mean,
obviously things change, and sometimes changes can get confusing. That's what this next song's about. "

Amen, brother. You think I like these slacks I'm wearing? I'm
going through some pretty confusing changes myself — trust
me. These hair highlights or whatever they're called were supposed to be cool, bleached-out streaks like the ones Anthony
Kiedis from Red Hot Chili Peppers had.

They start into the next number — something about a lover
changing his mind about loving and how it hurts emotionally.
I'm just staring at the carpet and counting the little squares
in the pattern, trying to keep my mind off of this song, but
occasionally I squint a little while tilting my head, so it looks
like I'm thinking about the music. I am shifting my focus from
the carpet, and up to the leg of the chair, then after looking
at that for a minute, I stare at the base of the lamp. Suddenly
I can't help but think, *Is Vallerie okay with this? Didn't she go
through a big breakup pretty recently? She's beautiful. I mean,
everyone is, but . . .* It takes everything in me not to walk
across the room and hold my boss in my arms, sway her to the
beat, and tell her that everything is going to be all right for all
of us.

The song finally finishes. Dude has another little rap to say
as a closing thing. Something about, "Thanks for the opportunity to be here today, we have no idea what comes next, so
we're just going to try to stay true to what we do."

Look, dude, here is maybe the real reason that I can't listen
too closely to the songs you've written: All I can think about

is what a huge day this is for you, and it would be for me, too, and every friend I've ever had: a record company has plucked you from the masses of hopefuls, and flown you to the New York office so you could play for us today. I envy you deeply, seriously. I'm not trying to be smartass. It's a pretty huge thing, any way you cut it, to stick it out until record companies are forced to pay attention. But I've only been here a relatively short time and I've already seen the likes of you disappear before you even had a chance to get out there and do what you do. I mean, they blow all of this smoke, they talk you up like this. They sign you to a contract, and they fly you out to play in the office or at a club. And maybe your record will come out. A lot of times it doesn't. A lot of times, believe it or not, it winds up on a shelf and you're trapped in a contract. But if it does come out, and if it sells less than five hundred thousand copies, every vice president or copresident that is kissing your ass in the offices today will act like it wasn't their idea to sign the guys that fell short of selling a million. So in a way, it's like you were singing in your song there, I'm afraid to get my heart into this and be made to look like I was stupid for being the guy who was trying to believe.

They're done playing their songs. I look to Dick to see if there will be any closing remarks, or if we're free to leave. He's quietly looking at them to make sure they've stopped, but when he realizes they're done, he just kind of looks up at us like, "Hmmm . . . interesting." He doesn't say anything. None of us do. Aging Suburban Classic Rock Guy starts to make a slow move for the door, loudly whispering to nobody in particular something about a conference call. A phone rings out in front of Vallerie's office and Amy excuses herself to grab it. Vallerie is looking at me like she has an assignment to talk to me about. In my head, I pretend the songs have moved her as much as they did me, and she wants to talk to me about love. She picks up the phone, getting distracted by the call. We all file out in silence and I tell myself everyone's quietly thinking thoughts like *The heart is a fragile thing* and *I will never make sense of life; so finite, bittersweet, and over too quickly, no matter when it ends* as we walk briskly back to our offices to finish the day.

Before We Move On, a Record-Business Riddle

Q: How many of the likes of us does it take to change a light
    bulb?

A: First of all, before we change anything, is the light bulb really
    burned out? Maybe we just need to breathe some life into it;
    repackage it, maybe the light bulb could do a duet with some-
    body (Sheryl Crow? Tim McGraw?) in hopes of getting some
    crossover appeal, maybe it could be in a beer commercial,
    maybe we could get it out on the road with a brighter light
    bulb. The other thing to think about is that this summer, Honda
    is rolling out a $100 million campaign for a new car aimed at
    thirty-somethings who consider themselves adventurous/
    spontaneous but can't really afford something like a luxury
    SUV and it might be a perfect campaign to tie this light bulb
    into, at least it would be the perfect demographic, in terms
    of age.

    Also, and this is just an idea: what if we found out what
    video games are being released in the third quarter and maybe
    pitch the idea of having our light bulb make an appearance in
    the video game at some certain level of completion; like, you
    get to a dark cave, let's say, if it's an adventure game, and if
    you have enough points, you can get the light bulb — and it
    would be our light bulb, obviously — and then it's easier to
    see in the cave. The other thing is this: worst-case scenario,
    the light bulb is, in fact, burned out. Is that really the end of
    the world? I mean, maybe that's actually of more value to us
    in the long run. Picture this for voiceover: "The light bulb is
    dead . . . but the legend lives on . . . rereleased, remastered,
    revealed . . . the light bulb . . . *in stores now.*" It almost makes
    more sense than taking the time changing it, plus, if it's dead

we can sell it without dealing with it, you know what I mean? No demands from it, no hotels, no road expense, no delays in the project from its end, etc. But, like I said, I'm just thinking off the top of my head here, just brainstorming, and none of this is written in stone. But the first thing we should do is figure out how we want to handle this, because the light bulb's manager is a total nightmare and we're going to have to take a meeting and listen to him sooner or later, and we should know what our plan is before we sit down with him. And let me tell you right now that the first thing out of his mouth is going to be, "This light bulb should be the brightest light bulb in the world, and it could be the brightest light bulb in the world, but you need to support the light bulb, you need to give the light bulb TV ads, you need to be more active in giving the light bulb tour support, we need to have some promotion from your end!" and on and on. And in that meeting, if you're in it, the only answer from our side should be that we're obviously very excited to be working with the light bulb, that we don't think it needs to be changed, that the only problem is people haven't seen how bright the light bulb could be, and our plan is to do everything we can to make this light bulb happen.

I'll send out an e-mail to everyone before the meeting to remind people of our position on this, but the bottom line is we don't have the budgets right now, and basically we need to see something happening with the light bulb before we go throwing good money after bad, but obviously we can't have the light bulb's manager hearing that. I can tell you all that I'm personally very excited to be working with the light bulb, I think it will light up very brightly, and we're not going to stop working the light bulb, in whatever ways budgets will permit, until it does, in fact, light up very brightly. . . . The light bulb is a very big priority for us from the top of the company to the bottom. Period. We can talk more about this when I am back from Barbados next week, and I'm going to need everybody's help on this. I know we can do it, but we need everybody working hard.

How to Shoot a Three-Hundred-Pound Hip-Hop Star from the Bronx

Vallerie asks me to write a treatment for the new Fat Joe commercial. I find myself writing some totally over-the-top gangster thug scene that would cost way too much to shoot. Partly because I'm over-compensating for feeling like a timid white guy in a pretty little office, nervous to be writing a thirty-second TV commercial treatment that's going to be sent to a South Bronx gangsta-rap icon who spits rhymes about life on the streets. And yes, maybe the other reason is that the more over-the-top the scenario I write, the more it will cost to shoot, and I'll be off the hook from directing said three-hundred pound, totally intimidating South Bronx gangsta-rap icon, and able to make a simple TV commercial by editing something together from his music video. The only problem with my big plan is that Fat Joe (aka Joey Crack in the old days) loves my treatment.

"He loves it. Hands down *loves* your idea!" Vallerie says with a sense of glee that, after growing up with an older sister, I have come to recognize as lovingly sinister.

"Yeah, well, it would cost so much to shoot, so, you know. I mean, the location alone. I mean, I've got him in something called 'hip-hop headquarters high above the city, with power-mogul-thug panoramic windows,'" I say in hopes I will dissuade her from the whole idea.

"A location will cost us nothing! I've already put a call into Ahmet's assistant saying you'll need to scout out his office as a possible location. They said you can go up there this afternoon and check it out."

Ah, nice. Yeah, that is a perfect first impression to make on a legend in this business. Good then, Ahmet Ertegun — the man who signed John Coltrane, who's arguably responsible for bringing black music to white America, who started Atlantic Records with a eight- or ten-thousand-dollar loan from his dentist in 1947 to watch it become one of the most influential record labels in America during the sixties and seventies — he'll be on the lookout for the guy from marketing who wants to make his perfectly respectable office into something called a hardcore hip-hop headquarters with power-mogul thug windows. Charmed, I'm sure. I can see it already:

"Hello, sir, yes, yes, nice to meet you. Finally. Wow. None of us would even be here without you. You're a legend — more of a rock star than today's so-called rock stars. You signed everyone from Ray Charles and Aretha Franklin to Led Zeppelin and the Rolling Stones. Ahem . . . okay, well, little bit about me, sir. Uh, let's see; been here a number of months now. You may recognize some of my work — 'Don't Bring a Gun to School'? That ring a bell at all? It was a public service announcement? With the Donnas? Uh, let's see . . . 'twenty-five'? That was a Phil Collins print ad. Anyway, could I just get you to move your coffee table, sir, that's where I want to have some bitches and hoes hanging out. I might have one of my thug's posse knocking boots with a ho on your sofa there, as well, because that's a real nice couch. That looks expensive; could really say 'hip-hop mogul' if I dress it up a little. And if you could move some of the things off your desk for me, that'd be great. Great place for the bling and ice an' shit that I'd like to have laying around this crib; big platinum piece with a bunch of diamonds that says Terror Squad on it. Frankly, sir, I see nothing but possibilities in here, the way you've set things up."

I have never been more terrified of an idea of mine getting the green light.

———————

That afternoon, I go upstairs to see his office. He's not in, but his assistant meets me in front of his office. She walks me over and lets me go in and look around. She stands at the door while keeping an eye on me. The desk is immaculate. Huge and solid and square, and everything on it placed perfectly in order.

"And we could move, just maybe that stack of papers off of his desk, right? We would want just a clear shot of . . ."

"Oh, no, no. I don't think you could really move any of the papers."

Right . . . okay, that answers my next question about rigging the ceiling with lights, moving the couch up against the window so the skyline's in the background, running steel tracking for the camera from the door and up to that desk, and basically having about fifteen crew people with walkie-talkies walking around in here. Fact is, I knew the second I walked in here and saw this place that there was no way we could ever invade this place. But I'm sure this as close as I'll ever get to the legend that started all this. I'm just some ad guy working in the marketing department and I'm pretty damn certain that isn't the kind of guy who gets a formal introduction to Ahmet Ertegun. Hands politely clasped behind my back — remember to use the kind of posture that my parents taught me to have for special occasions when I was a little kid. I feel like I should start asking her more logical questions about the office since my only other option seems to be to gaze upon all of this with my mouth wide open until I get goosebumps and start weeping openly.

Look at these photos on the table between the couches. Here he is with Mick Jagger and Jerry Hall. Here's one with Led Zeppelin way back in the day — this might be the actual day he signed them; the day that was responsible for eventually getting *Led Zeppelin IV* into the world and eventually into my sister's suburban bedroom so I could sneak it out and listen. Wait, are they sitting on these same couches in the photo? I walk over to a wall lined with photographs from a lifetime of friendships with everyone you can think of, from musical legends to diplomats and presidents. Look at this, a framed royalty accounting statement from one of the first Ray Charles records, typewritten through a carbon and sent to his attention. Even the texture of this wall says something. Put your face close to it. Feel that? It's almost a fabric, isn't it? Get close to the smell of it, smell this world where walls feel almost like a thick parchment, a world where America is still . . .

"Okay, so, did you have any other questions, or . . ."

She's still standing behind me watching.

"Right, anyway, I'm just looking at the, uh, wall here, making sure it would work if, uh . . . Yes, yes, that's good. That would work. Good. Okay, well, thank you. Thanks for, you know, letting me . . . okay, thank you."

———

Of course the location for my hip-hop TV commercial does not end up being Ahmet Ertegun's office. The location turns out to be this guy's office on the next floor down. Vallerie meets me there to unlock it and let me in. Nice place, pretty big corner office with one of those, like, twenty- or thirty-thousand-dollar stereo systems with all the tube amps and everything; oddly, there's no music next to it. No photos of anyone anywhere, either. No framed notes or letters, nothing more personal than a very expensive collection of furniture and lighting that looks like a permanent installment at a museum of modern art in any key U.S. city. This place already feels like a set; like a façade.

"Wow, nice. Whose office is this?"

"Some guy who told someone at Warners about Madonna, or knew Madonna way back in the day and told her to sign with them, or knew her manager . . . something. Anyway, he comes in, honestly, maybe once or twice a month. This place just kind of sits here for him. He'll probably never even know you had a shoot in here," Vallerie says.

Over the next week, a camera crew is hired up, and this guy's office is completely converted. The furniture's moved out of the way; all of Fat Joe's gold and platinum record awards are sent over; the big Terror Squad diamond piece is delivered; a metal briefcase filled with fake cash is brought in and lit perfectly; instantly these big huge floor-to-ceiling velvet drapes are brought in to adorn all windows; dolly track is laid down from the door to the desk for the opening shot, light rigging clogs and lines the ceiling; more furniture is moved out; angles are cheated; monitors are set up so I can see the shot — none of this, of course, is done by me. Foot soldiers from the video production department have made this whole scene a reality, propping me up to be applauded and probably paid a bigger Christmas bonus.

Fat Joe and his posse arrive. My God, this is how it should be. There is so much love and loyalty between these guys. I think to myself: *I don't know why white people can't be more like this. We need the nicknames and handshakes . . . more embraces!*

I check around to make sure there are food and drinks. Our stingy little budget has allowed for a deli tray of cold cuts, some sliced fruit, and cheeses for this huge man and his wife and posse of lifelong friends. And with a smile and a laugh, he changes all that and it goes something like this:

"What's this shit we got here, B?"

(B?)

"Oh, well, have some cheese, and grapes and things here. That's for you; for all of you, so help yourselves. But then let's try a run through of . . ."

"We gonna call and get some real food up in here first." He yells into the next room to his wife: "Honey! Let's get some barbecue up in here from [name unintelligible]. And find out what everybody wants for drinks, all they got over here now is some little cheese cubes an' shit."

Oh, my God, they're laughing at the deli trays. These guys rule! I haven't wanted to be somebody's friend this badly since I was seven.

"Yeah, thing is the budget the label has for this whole shoot is really only . . ."

"This breaks the bank, then you have 'em call Joe. They got my phone number and if somebody's sweatin' it you have 'em call me, a'ight, B?"

I'm not supposed to be calling him B back, right?

"Yeah. Yeah! Call barbecue up. Up here. Get some up in here."

Right on! This is feeling like some kind of super feel-good
Disney script where the suburban white geek finds a new
friend in a huge gangster hip guy with a heart of gold.

"Call them. I know, look at this!" I add, maybe too excitedly.

A very sobering look from one of his right-hand men.
Mean-looking guy, too. Holy shit, what's his nickname? They
should call him "Killer" or "The Executioner" or something
heavy like that. Still locked in on me with the glare just because I agreed with Fat Joe about the fruit tray or whatever?
Jesus, relax, dude. He's still your friend, okay? God.

I walk into the conference room across the hall from where
Fat Joe is to see if any of his guys need any help getting the
TV tuned into cable or anything. Smoke. The room is filled
with it. It must be something electrical. Quick! Get a fire ex-
tinguisher. Wait. Are they smoking pot? In the conference
room? You can't just go smoking pot in the conference room!
Can you smoke pot in the conference room? Not cool! Not
cool at all!

Okay, I'm cool with it.

It's cool, it's cool, alright.

I'm down with it, no big deal.

Pot's no big deal.

Shit, stop staring at them.

You're staring at them.

Stop it, you look uptight.

It's illegal, though.

Whatever.

Apparently I've stood here stunned too long and it looks
like I want some. And now the mean looking dude is holding
it out toward me. Be cool about it.

"Nah, I'm all set. Thanks, though. Thanks." Okay shut up.

The food comes and one of the foot soldiers from video production pays the tab with cash and gets a receipt. It's like a big cookout up here. The shoot is almost secondary to all of them getting together, high and laughing, telling stories about the neighborhood back in the day, watching the Knicks game on the TV, talking about the record business and what's happening and how it didn't used to be that way, talking about how it's gonna be. I wish these guys worked here.

We get to shooting the commercial for his new album. And the whole idea to this thirty-second-long commercial is that we see Fat Joe sitting behind this huge desk in this gorgeous piece of prime Manhattan real estate. A briefcase of cash on the table, a light in front of him, but he's sitting back and his face is in a dramatic shadow. The camera tracks up toward him. When I give him the cue, he leans in and says the name of his new album, *Loyalty.* That's the whole idea; camera moves through huge corner of prime Manhattan real estate, we see the platinum albums on the wall, the diamonds on the table, the briefcase filled with cash, and large man sitting behind a huge desk; the large man behind the huge desk leans forward out of the shadow and into the light, we see that the man is Fat Joe, and he simply says the word *Loyalty.* The viewer of this commercial will then see an album cover that has a picture of Fat Joe on it and the word *Loyalty.* The viewer will then say to themselves, "Ah, I see the new Fat Joe album is titled *Loyalty.* I would expect it to be available in stores now." If there is any doubt in the viewer's mind, an announcer's voiceover will say, "*Loyalty.* The new album from Fat Joe. In stores now."

I sit down at the little monitor, put a pair of headphones on, and we try the first one. I'm watching the shot unfold and I've just realized I'm not going to be able to sit here silent.

"Cut! Okay, Joe, don't tap your foot like that, because I'm seeing it in the bottom of the shot. Let's do it again."

"Okay, yeah, won't do that. Sorry."

Whoa. No way. That was so easy. He was so kind and professional about that.

"And it's important that you lean forward when we get to the end of the shot. When we push all the way in, we need your face in the light just in front of you."

"Ah, yeah. Some kinda Scarface shit, right, B? B knows how to do this shit, let's go!"

As we run through a few more takes, I have that moment we all have at different points in our lives; that moment where you see a side of yourself you've yet to meet. And it turns out, I really kind of like telling huge hip-hop kingpins what to do. There's a bit of charge in that for a white guy with middling confidence. I start coming up with a lot of great things to add on when I say "Cut."

"Cut! Okay, remember, I don't know who's in the shadow yet, Joe. The first time we're seeing you should be when you lean in. Alright, people, let's do another one!"

The camera starts back at its first position and I can't help thinking, *Ooh, I have to say that little part at the end where I say, "Alright, people! that was nice."* We continue shooting a few more takes and I've got a nice assortment of things to say that I must've picked up watching *Inside the Actors Studio* or something, because they sound perfect. I've got, "Cut! I'm still seeing a hot spot when the camera hits the mark, can somebody check that?" and I also trot out a little number that goes, "Cut! That was beautiful, let's do one more like that, but Joe, don't be in a hurry to say the line. You're running the show here, you're taking your own sweet time to speak up — don't make the move in a hurry for the camera, you don't care about the camera. Okay, everybody, let's go again, please."

When we're done shooting the commercial, they're gone. Just like that, which seems so fast for all of the work leading up to it, but I guess come to think of it, once you actually get around to it, it doesn't take too long to get five, ten, or fifteen takes of one thirty-second shot, for one thirty-second TV commercial, featuring one guy, saying one word. And just as quickly as Fat Joe and his posse arrived, they recede into the night. I walk over to the window and look down from way up here; an aerial view of the Range Rover and Mercedes caravan leaving at the bottom of the building. It snakes its way past Radio City Music Hall and Rockefeller Plaza, rolling out of view and off to all of the places I imagine them showing up. I head back to my office and fill out one of those voucher things so a sensible luxury sedan will come to take me home.

INAPPROPRIATE GREETINGS AND SALUTATIONS FOR MIDDLE-AGED WHITE RECORD EXECUTIVES TO EXCHANGE

1. Hello, Dawg.
2. What is up, my niggaz?
3. Respec (*sic*).
4. True dat.
5. Steve from accounts payable is a hater, yo.

POSITIVELY FIFTY-SECOND STREET:
A FIELD GUIDE TO A FEW OF THE SPECIES
I'VE SPOTTED HERE IN THE OFFICE

The Heavy Hitter

You're making seven figures. You're probably responsible for some label's big superstar's success. Or maybe you're just good at convincing people you're responsible for some label's big superstar's success. On the low end, the books probably show a high six- or low-seven-figure salary, but it's no secret that the bonuses would most likely double or triple that each year. What confuses me about you guys is how credibility varies wildly amongst you — there are the good apples; met one once that was asking to take a zero salary until things turned around in the business, was saying he was fine taking one for the team by setting aside his salary and just getting paid on his acts' records if they sold. But there's the other kind of apples, too — I saw one of you in the elevator just before you got put on the cut list. I was riding up to some meeting. You got on the elevator with the co-whatever. Copresident, cochairman, co-something. You were still intact in the company, in control, in the money, still in the big corner office upstairs, in well with everybody. The Co-Guy was talking to you, and I was the ghost standing there overhearing the whole thing. And since everyone's so good at ignoring each other in the elevator, you guys just talked like I wasn't there. Your partner told you there was nothing to worry about, said something like, "I think we look fine, and I don't think there's anything you need to worry about. Honestly." Of course, three weeks later you were a grown man literally weeping as your assistants started bubble-wrapping everything in your huge corner office. Whoops, turns out you had something to worry about after all.

Upper Management

You lurk in the same places; same corner offices, same executive washrooms. But instead of seven figures, you're grossing well into six. You haven't signed anyone, but maybe you have, like, an other-worldly hunch for picking hit singles for radio from an album of nine filler songs with two made-for-radio singles. You make your picks after the two songs have been tested to death by independent research firms whom the label pays to call random everyday people up on the telephone, play them a short section of the song, then ask them if they like it or not. The firm then tells you which one is statistically bound to be a hit. Sometimes they even use computer programs to analyze characteristics of the song. How long is the chorus? What's the chord progression? How long till we get to the chorus? How many beats per minute is the song recorded at? At any rate, when the research comes in telling you what song is statistically most likely bound to be a hit, you then pick that song as the first single to be serviced to radio stations. I may be missing something here, but am pretty sure that covers your day in your corner office. I know you're on the phone a lot, so there might be a little more to it.

Glorified Middle Manager

Smaller office, sure. And you're using the regular old nonexecutive washroom, so you're not making small talk with influential cohorts while you urinate, a peculiar thrill that you've not yet come to know. You do anything from producing music videos to spending your days convincing VH1 and MTV to play the music video from the forthcoming album, even though something like 78 percent of MTV's programming is reality shows as opposed to music videos. You're probably kissing the two-hundred-grand mark and you might even be a ways north of that. If you're not, well, at least you get to tell your friends that you took a six-figure gig since they're certainly giving you anywhere from a hundred to a hundred and seventy-five plus bonuses. If you're super savvy, you've got your own little business incorporated and you can make even more money by invoicing the company additional fees for creative and production services that are mutually regarded as above and beyond your day-to-day job. Yes, we see that you've got the newest Blackberry. Now. Put. It. Down.

Glorified Foot Soldier

You're basically on the same program as the Glorified Middle Manager, but the only catch is, you can't manage anyone, so you probably wouldn't survive in any other corporate environ. You may not survive in this one. While you can't manage others, you have this weird little way of keeping to yourself and creating things when told. And sometimes the things you create generate money for the company by way of increased sales. Advertising, maybe the random idea born in weekend isolation, maybe a way to market a band that won't do them in. Sometimes you write the copy for Holiday Gift Guides for the November issues of women's magazines that feature a paid advertisement/holiday gift guide about the best holiday records, which all happen to be issued by the company you're working for (surprise). And you write the guide in such a way that your bosses actually see a sales spike. Your low self-esteem tells you that the sales spike is seasonal and dependable, no matter who writes about the albums. Anyway, your talents are unremarkable enough to keep you largely anonymous at the upper reaches of the company, and enough of a justified expense to keep you well paid, which leads to the harder-working and way lesser-paid foot soldiers resenting you.

So your life is a charming mix of benign obscurity and walking around feeling the weight of stares that make you feel like a voodoo doll full of pins. The Glorified Foot Soldier is a lonely little soldier that way.

Real Foot Soldier

Who was there when, say, slow-jam diva Brandy needed new clothes brought to her hotel room in the snow storm? Or some gangster princess hip-hop starlet was freaking out because she thought her arms looked fat in the scenes where she's wearing a leather corset in her video? You! You're the real deal, because you actually *do* something. Truth is, you work harder than practically everyone above you and make way less. Understand these things:

1. You're connected to the culture that the company pays through the nose to try and understand, because you are a card-carrying member of that generation.
2. You're more connected to the word on the street and bands than almost everyone above you in the company, though they are being overpaid to act like they understand.
3. The older people working above you at the label are, in most cases, intimidated by you (see points one and two). Here's another thing you should be let in on: they know you are worth way more money and that they're getting you on the cheap, and they go to great lengths to never let you realize any of this. Whoops. Now I've done it. Cat's out of the bag. Well, since I gave away the big secret, maybe you should ask for a raise. Oh, I forgot, there's a line of three hundred people who, for some reason, are willing to do your job for less or even as an unpaid intern. Does this baffle you? This baffles me, too. Hang in there.

You've Got an Idea, and the Only Problem with That Is This: Ideas Make the Robots Attack

These days, between the hours of eleven PM and about two or three AM, I'm wide awake downloading music and scribbling notes like a gainfully employed, insomniac version of Dustin Hoffman in *Rainman,* or an overzealous and barely rehabilitated middle-aged delinquent trying to turn over a new leaf with night classes.

I'm seduced away from sleep by the idea that, between the new Apple laptop the company bought me and the high-speed wireless Internet access in the apartment, there's essentially a record store in every room. I've got another monkey on my back, sister. The only reason I even get around to falling asleep at all is because at a certain point I give in to a particularly dreamy section of a song blasting in my headphones and drift off to sleep in the living room. I defy you to listen to any of the huge, brooding, genius, beautiful, and haunting songs by Mogwai in AKG K240 headphones at three in the morning without next waking up tangled in headphone cords, in a panic because you're late for work. The scribbling of notes makes it somehow seem like I'm a go-getter adult man applying due diligence to his office job, and less like it's an addiction or disorder — my girlfriend is impressed, as opposed to concerned about my lack of self-control; not staring or judging . . . *admiring.* The notes are observations about my new music consumption habits, sentences and thoughts at once embarrassing, ambitious, confused, disjointed, but strangely and surprisingly well-organized. And one night at around 3:40 AM it hits me, I'm confronted with it, there's no denying it, no covering it up; I take the first step and admit it: I've got an idea. A what? Yes! An idea!

And this pile of notes, over a period of a month or two of staying up late downloading music, cooks down into a seven- or eight-page presentation. I give it to Vallerie, who sends it up to a copresident as well as a senior vice-something. The most groundbreaking, mind-blowing part of this idea is probably the way it speeds upward into the top reaches of the company at breakneck speed; a nosebleed-inducing ascent. I start thinking it's a sting operation; that they're going to get me into the conference room with the copresidents and then sue me for downloading music. I have already planned out a defense, telling them the truth: Larry, a VP in marketing, is the one that told me about Limewire and helped me install it on my work laptop. I didn't even want it at first, but he told me it was the most incredible thing. He told me how you can find files of anything and you don't have to go through the hassle of ripping CDs, and he was right! I only wanted to try it once, but I got hooked my first night using it! Almost instantly I was as excited about music as I was when I was nine, searching and downloading and sharing every night. And only weeks after Larry hooked me up with Limewire, Warner Music's legal department sent our entire staff an e-mail saying that the RIAA was going to start suing people, and that if any of us had any illegal downloading applications such as Limewire on our work or personal computers, we should uninstall them. I disregarded that e-mail. And now this! A sting. I knew something was up. I've got the usual symptoms of your basic good old-fashioned jitters — some difficulty performing minor everyday tasks; physical coordination giving way occasionally to spasmodic movement and a stilted gait; auditory hallucinations; the edges of the lips and tips of the fingers turn a pale blue; heart and respiratory rates become arrhythmic while a high fever persists, loss of depth perception sets in, and a brittle crackling sound can be easily detected in the lungs without the use of a stethoscope.

"Did they call you about your idea?" This from Vallerie, popping her head into my office.

"His assistant, yeah. They're going to call me back. Set something. Up."

"He's probably going to want you to walk everyone through it in their meeting next week!" she says.

"Fuck."

"What?"

"Good."

The day of the meeting rolls around quickly, like a blur. I'm starting to catch on to the fact that whenever something happens in a blur, it's almost always bad. When you trip and fall on your face, it happens in a blur. Heavy machinery on Midwestern farms claims limbs in a blur — wars, dubious recounts favoring the Bush administration, regrettable one-night stands in your twenties with unconventionally attractive community-college students usually battling depression and living like hobos, late-night checking-account debits that you wake up remembering — all of these things happen in a blur.

I walk next door, over to 75 Rockefeller Plaza. The address that was written at the very bottom of the records I would sit in front of the family stereo or my plastic record player and listen to when I was a kid. That was what we all did back then: listen to the songs, stare at every picture of the band on the sleeve and cover while tracing every single line of small print, eventually moving past song titles, names of guys in the band, publishing credits, photo credits, and eventually down the little nine-point line of type that was this address. I push my way through the revolving door. Up the elevator, then out to wander down the hall to this conference room, distracted by wondering what it was like up here way back in the day.

I heard it was incredible and strange here at 75 Rock; that the Rolling Stones had been given an entire floor of offices as part of their deal back then. Can you imagine a floor governed by the Rolling Stones and their management? Smoke, drink, do whatever you want, or whatever the sexy six-foot-one-inch reprobate stripper/groupie person living in your office wants to do. Take a shot of Jack from the bottle on your desk, take a shot at the photocopy machine with whatever firearm is laying next to the bottle of Jack on your desk. That's the way I imagine it while I daydream my way down the hall toward this meeting. I wonder if Led Zeppelin ever wandered this hallway. Every corridor I walk down, every gold or platinum record on the wall, feels like walking through the background of one of those little tiny black-and-white photographs they used to have in the seventies rock magazines of my youth, like *Circus* and *Creem*. Those little snapshots of a rock star flanked by three guys in suits, and maybe one guy in a satin jacket with a band name or label's logo on it. It would look like the rock star was being hassled for back taxes by a cluster of IRS agents, save for the fact that everyone in the shot would be laughing and smiling; especially the guys in the suits.

Walking into the conference room, I see everyone except the copresident who invited me to this. A whole new group, a whole different department, really. These guys are from the A&R department (Artist and Repertoire), these are the people who scout out bands and sign them to contracts. The only person in the group whom I recognize somewhat is Angry New Media Chick and her sidekick guy. I've seen her around occasionally. I remember her from that day recording public service announcements with the Donnas. She's maybe late thirties and tired looking, makes a lot of money ushering record executives through the age of the Internet, and seems fueled mostly by resentment masked with stale congeniality. But more than anything, it's her hair that precedes her. It's crazy-person hair, no matter how you cut it. It is hair that says, "I'd much rather be sleeping late in an abandoned loft where I'm free to smoke menthol cigarettes in a second-hand terry-cloth bathrobe, sitting on a saggy couch, while I comment to nobody in particular about the people on a reality television show like they're my family." Or maybe I'm projecting again.

Everyone sits at the conference table with a printout of my idea in front of them, looking a bit bored, somehow not quite as excited as I imagined them looking. I do my polite, professional office grin — a slight turning up of the corners of the mouth, combined with nod downward — while silently mouthing a combination of the words "hey" and "hello." They kind of do the office-grin back, but not really.

There's a forty-two-inch high-definition plasma screen hanging on the wall to my right, and the screen is filled with more people. Whoa! Video connection to the conference room at the Los Angeles office. Slightly more tan than us, unless maybe the tint or color setting is off, but clearly waiting just as plainly nonplussed. We all sit there looking at a picture of each other, bored on both coasts. Someone in the room asks me if this printout in front of each person is my idea, and I say yes, unable to take my eyes off the plasma-screen people. I do a little hello-nod to the people on screen, almost a secret one to see if maybe one person might catch it and respond. Nobody does. I barely raise my hand an inch or two off the table and do a tiny, hesitant and fast wave with three fingers to see if they'll notice. One guy on-screen who seems to be looking right at me suddenly looks down, but maybe this is coincidence though? Through the speakers in the ceiling, I can hear him shuffle the handout three thousand miles west of here. We all continue waiting silently on both coasts.

The big guy we've been waiting on shows up. Co-Man, who aside from being a co-something is the cohead of A&R. Like a day's magic hour that is neither quite twilight or dusk, Co-Man is magic-age; not thirty, not forty, not fifty; simply high-energy, clean-cut, well groomed, exfoliated, moisturized, braced and energized by a good herbal toning and revitalizing tonic — and dressed pointedly casual in a T-shirt and jeans that somehow still indicate a premium price point befitting of the seven-figure income.

Suddenly everyone is animated; everyone one is flipping through the papers in front of them; faces are alive instead of dormant; the little bored people on the video screen are smiling and adjusting their seats, as if they're characters in a video game that has finally been reset; the instant burst of life catches me by surprise and leads to the mild confusion of suddenly feeling invigorated and hopeful. The meeting starts. Mostly the first round is dedicated to the usual business of the

A&R department: Who are you listening to that you like? How are their club shows selling? Are they selling a lot of merchandise at their shows? Are any other labels looking at them? Has anyone else here heard them? And after enough of that, the big guy holds up the handout of the idea. The idea!

The idea, I should tell you at this point, is not rocket science. It's basically a proposal for a new type of contract that would be used to sign developing artists to a digital deal on online-release-only terms. In short, it would let the label release a band's work digitally for a smaller advance than the standard contract, and secure the rights to first refusal when it comes to releasing it in other formats such as CDs, soundtracks, and so on, if the songs do well in an online release. And without boring you to death, basically the big thing about it is that even though we're talking about an online-only release, there's a way that the idea keeps a foot in traditional retail outlets. And traditional retail outlets are eroding as I type this, and there are points in the execution of this online-only idea that address staying in touch with the consumer as they migrate away from standard retail. The other big thing about it is that it has this way of approaching the label's back catalog in the marketing of developing artists. And frankly, I'm not so sure why I'm being so vague about describing it to you, because if I'm fired tomorrow, there are fifty handouts left here in this building with every detail about how the idea works, fifty handouts printed up and plagued with phrases like "Consumers migrating from brick-and-mortar retail and looking for options aside from the iTunes Music Store" are all written out and sitting in front of everyone. I call this little digital label Buzz Share, which, yes, is pretty much the lamest name ever.

Co-Man introduces me and this time I do bigger nods to the people in front of me, and a full-size wave to the people on screen.

"Okay, so I know I sent this to everyone kind of last-minute, I think there's something here. I think it's an idea we should be investigating, but I want to know what you guys think about it."

Holy God! A bicoastal Greek chorus of things like this:

"Yeah, we should definitely be moving in this direction. I like the thinking behind this. I would use it."

"We should be looking at this. I'm not sure exactly how we start to implement it, but it's something we should be trying."

Goddamn, I wish this guy could hold up everything I've ever said, done, thought, or written so I could just bathe in the kind of instant validation he commands. Anything he holds up in front of the camera is praised.

"Here's a speeding ticket Dan from marketing got when he was nineteen. He was going eighty-five in a forty-five, plus passing two vehicles on the right. I think he was on to something with his thinking, but I want to know what you guys think," the big guy might say. And then the people in the meeting and on the screen would shine a new light on this incident, and they'd baptize me with praise:

"I love it. I don't see it as reckless driving. I see it as *ambitious* driving."

"I like his thinking here. Using the shoulder of the highway to pass is inventive."

Then he'd hold up the next item for everyone to see: "Here's a Polaroid that a security officer took of him unconscious in a job interview he blew back when he still drank and partied. He literally passed out in the middle of the interview after an all-nighter of excess and not being able to find the right combination of various stimulants and gin to take the edge off completely that morning." And again, I would sit being redeemed by their replies:

"Some people would've call him a derelict for passing out in a job interview, but I can't help but see this as the ability to shift the paradigm of the interview process. I like his thinking here."

Someone else might speak up, "Whose fault is it that he's asleep? That's the question I would ask. He wasn't being engaged, and I think that falls on the shoulders of the company interviewing him."

After the requisite amount of employees agreeing and championing the idea, the big guy introduces a small devil's advocate point.

He says something to effect of: "Well, it's not a hands-down perfect idea. One big thing we'll need to talk about, we'll need to figure out, is who runs this, because it would kind of be a new division. Is it a separate department or is it folded into New Media?"

Uh oh . . . Angry New Media Chick keyed in on that little phrase and is stirring in her seat like she's ready to launch. She stirs again, Co-Man looks her way, and she sends the first warhead my way:

"Look, you can't come in here making more work for my department! You're basically saying our Web site has no role in [words, words, words, words, words]. You can't just decide you [more words, coupled with awkward angry rant about needing to take responsibility for my ideas, etc. Words, words, various angry faces.]."

"No . . . I'm not saying . . . I think the Web site is great. I'm not even talking about that. This would be a totally separate thing. I mean. No. I like . . . I mean . . . your department is awesome. Or."

Thinking: *Jesus, did Co-Man set me up for this slaughter just to get Vallerie to quit asking him about my idea or something?*

There are two people representing the media department — her and this guy who's boisterous and also angry, albeit in a more innocent, less aggressive, more "Keiffer Sutherland character who really wants to stress that he's not happy" kind of way. Anyway, they both make great money, and it seems like anytime they think they're going to have to do more than maintain the company site they start screaming dot-com words that the senior vice president co-people don't understand. And they've got an awesome corner on things, since we're talking about a place where anyone above middle management has to yell to their assistants for help with something as technical as, say, an e-mail attachment. So, yeah, it's totally taking-candy-from-babies time. Anyway, I've seen Angry New Media Chick and Loud Man do this before.

> Executive: "Maybe we can figure out a way to make part of our site basically. . . ."
>
> ANMC: "Impossible! Back-end architecture! Cookies and lasers! Server-side technology!"
>
> LM will join in, too: "Yeah! What she said! Plus, I mean, I would have to see if what you're asking for is even feasible!"
>
> Executive: "Uh . . . okay."

Then you walk by Loud Man's office fifteen minutes later
and he's kicking back, has five Instant Message windows open
on his computer, his feet resting on one of the skateboards
that litter his office, one of his corporate groupies hanging
out on the couch reading a magazine or playing a video
game.

I quickly try to address these concerns of the project falling
on the New Media Department's shoulders.

Co-Man kind of looks over at them like, "Well?"

They start the rant of dot-com terminology to defend their
department from undertaking additional endeavors, let alone
developing ideas that will lead to an increased workflow. Eyes
glaze over. Terminology ricochets off the walls.

Jesus, fine. We get it. It can't be done.

They carry on a bit longer, and I totally lay back, unable to
defend. I'm killed by this mildly hysterical woman and her
angry man-friend who have mastered the aggressive board-
room shtick that I will never learn to do. I feel myself going
down, quiet and no longer interested in my idea as much as
I'm interested in how this small, angry man can kick my ass
so thoroughly. How do adults respond to this stuff in an office
environment? Can I hit him?

Part of me is thinking that if the copresident likes the idea
so much, I don't need to fight these New Media thugs trying to
remain in their stream of steady checks and fattening lunches,
do I?

The dust dies down; there are a few things left on the department's meeting agenda. I think Co-Man ends my segment
by saying something to the effect of, "Okay, well . . . we'll kind
of see how . . . yeah . . . good. So, next order of business."

After a few rounds of who's listening to what, the TV screen switches off, the people in Los Angeles fade away, and it feels like I disappear as well. We all file out, and I walk down the hall past those gold and platinum records again, this time feeling a little bit like an aged Beavis or Butt-head, thinking, "Uh, having a big idea, like, sucks or something."

Intuition Sells, but Who's Buying?

First off, in all fairness to Jewel: if I grew up without running water, an indoor bathroom, or television, only to then spend my formative years living in a van and bathing in public fountains so I could make some spare change by yodeling in coffeehouses — or whatever her story is — I would sell Schick one of my songs to advertise their new razor with. Period. And frankly, I wouldn't stop at letting Schick pay me seven figures to use my song as the soundtrack to their estimated forty-million-dollar ad campaign. I'd take things a step further, personally. I'd offer to paint the CEO's summerhouse for a fair price. I'd ask if the president of Schick's kids listened to my records. If the answer was yes, I'd be like, "Sweet, they'll freak when you bring home the shirt I'm wearing. It's the one I wore on the cover of the CD *and* in the video. Five grand, and you're a hero, Dad, come on. Right now. Make a move, or I'll just eBay it for more like eight grand." And I'd be peeling the shirt off of my back quicker than you can say "I'll never have to eat dented cans of shoplifted beans in my van again." Having said that, if I'd spent the last decade selling out tours behind twenty-five million records sold worldwide, I'd like to believe I'd think twice before letting Schick Corporation use one of my songs as an anthem for a women's razor.

But in today's sales and marketing meeting we're told that Jewel's working on a song for the upcoming album *0304* and that the song, "Intuition," bears the same name as this women's razor that Schick is bringing to market.

Little Loud Man from New Media pounces up from the middle left region of the conference table and commandeers the Dr. Evil huge-ass high-tech tabletop touch-screen audio/video command center. The speakers at the end of the room come to life. A little intro and beat and the first verse hits. Here's what Jewel starts to tell us in the song: She's basically telling us that she's a simple girl and that she's kind of stuck in this high-tech digital world. And she's saying she's really trying to understand what she describes as all of the powers — or people in charge — that rule this land.

(Okay, easy on the Phil Hartman Unfrozen Caveman Lawyer "I'm confused by your modern world" act, sister. You just worked with your label and management to corner yet another check equal to the Gross National Product of some of the countries your last six world tours swept you through, so, you kind of understand power.)

The song finds its groove. Aging Suburban Classic Rock Guy bobs his head as if he can't get enough of this one. A handful of aspiring co-somethings bob their heads as well and smile at each other. Anyone in the room who knows the irony of a song about not selling out being used to sell razors displays a perfect professional poker face. I, on the other hand, am most likely doing the thing where I stifle disbelief and then start getting paranoid that I totally don't understand what's going on and that it's showing on my face, and then I get paranoid that you can get cancer this way. I'm not sure what to use to tap to the beat, so I just fold my stupid long arms across my stomach. I don't know where to look, either, so I squint my eyes shut hard and try to focus on the song. An intern is kind enough to tap me on the shoulder and discreetly ask me if I am "having problems."

Jewel hits the chorus and tells us that we need to follow our hearts and follow our intuition and then kind of repeats that we only need follow our hearts, "Just follow your heart, baby," she sings out. The song is basically saying all this stuff about not giving into the insane waves of advertising and greed that are shoved at us all day long. But I still don't get it and feel like when I was little and they said they were going to have to hold me back a grade unless I got with the program. So, I'm really trying to get with the program. But, she just licensed this song about following your heart and not selling out for use in one of the biggest ad campaigns of the year. *Wait, maybe I'm dead and this is one of those old Disney comedies where I slowly start to realize I'm dead and nobody can see me except a child? And it's, like, a hundred years in the future and licensing folk singers' songs about not selling out for use in a forty-million-dollar ad campaign for razors makes sense to everyone in the future?*

I look around the room for any sign of somebody willing to clue me in so I can enjoy the meeting, too: the usual suspects are bobbing politely to the beat; a pair of daydreaming eyes is suddenly averted when I look right at them; one guy is politely drumming on the edge of the table with the stylus from his Palm Pilot.

The label is working to time the release of this CD and first single to the rollout of the Schick ad campaign. Which will coincide with the video for "Intuition," in which she'll portray characters such as "Firefighter" (red leather shorts, white tank top sprayed at when hot male models point their fire hose at her and soak her down) and "Soda Drinker" (drinks what appears to be popular brand of lemon-lime soda that makes her shirts pop open and her breasts heave forward while a wind blows back her hair), mocking a culture in which scantily clad pop divas embrace the notion that everything is for sale — but Jewel's, um, doing it in a way that is an irony, um, ironic. I'm confused.

I look over at the guy tapping his Palm Pilot stylus against the edge of the table. He's worked here for five or six years, from what I hear; huge office, doing really well, doing way better than I am. You ever have that feeling? The feeling that everyone else has figured this life out and is succeeding *wildly* while it feels like you're just doing okay or just getting by? That's the feeling I get watching this guy drumming to the song with his Palm Pilot stylus. What do I have to do to succeed wildly in this life?

I make a loose fist and start to kind of do a bass drum by tapping it on my binder, politely bobbing my head and smiling pleasantly as Jewel slides into the bridge and reveals the most telling line in the song: "Sell your sin, just cash in."

Sing it, sister.

SUBDIVISIONS

Sometimes I walk around the floors peeking in offices, like a tourist lost in a museum. You can't help but feel how this is your last chance to see this. That none of the old-school mogul stuff is going to last too much longer — a little slice of American pop culture that might've peaked and is now almost gone without a trace. You look into these dioramas of offices and see the people who've been here who knows how long — separated off in a world that seems so far away from the day-to-day goings on of the middle class. And the older, wealthier, and higher up they are in the managerial caste system, the older their hairstyle is. The biggest offices can be the strangest little time capsules — mostly the men's. The women seem to have an ability to move forward after their moment in the sun. The men, though . . . The guy who had something to do with discovering the band Rush twenty-five years ago apparently decided that very day that he would never change his hairstyle. The way a kid might declare that he would never wash his hand after meeting an absolutely peaking Evil Knievel in 1974.

When you walk by and look into the shadow box and see him sitting behind his huge desk and surveying his corner-office real estate like an isolated lord, you see a man who has been front and center for all of the highs, lows, hits, and stiffs of at least a couple of decades in this business. He looked up and smiled once as I was walking past stealing a glimpse, and I was stunned. This polite man behind such a huge desk in an enormous corner spread that looks bigger than a lot of apartments in this town — is he just a guy who learned the "smile and nod like a nice guy" trick? Because how the hell would a nice guy get anywhere in the record business? When you look in the couches, the huge living-room setting, the desk that is large enough to be called real estate, the art on the walls, the sculpture on the table in the center of the room, platinum albums lining the walls, each with their own little light focused on them — you see all this, but really, somehow, you keep coming back to the hair. When I learned that he's the man who found Rush, or knew Rush, or managed Rush or whatever his thing is — I felt this weird kind of reckless, quiet, almost teenage melancholy sweep over me; because barring a building fire or a relapse back into my days of heavy drinking, I knew I'd never talk with him about the good old days that must've occurred at some point in this business. Here's a guy who's got to have some of the coolest stories in this building, he seems like a nice guy, and I'll probably never hear his stories. I can't explain it, but you just don't talk to these guys, and they don't talk to you — even when it's just the two of you in the elevator for twenty-six floors.

There's always this sort of old-school-looking gym bag next to his desk and I daydream of how he arrived at the point where he decided that he would always have it next to his desk. Did it come later in his career, or was it one of those early-years crazy rock-and-roll contractual clauses? "Okay . . . a million three a year . . . a corner office . . . and a contract that says (1) I grab my gear and head to the club whenever I goddamn well please, (2) I never have to cut my hair, and (3) a hot

secretary brings me this gym bag and racquet anytime I press
this button on my phone . . . and the contract's pay or play for
the remainder of my employment or the next thirty years . . .
whichever is greater."

Back in the glory days of major labels, they wouldn't have
even wasted the time with meetings and getting approvals for
that kind of thing, I bet. All they would've been thinking was,
"This guy found Rush/knows Rush/signed Rush. We want
him. Give him *five* secretaries to bring him his tracksuit, headband, and racquet if that's what he wants. And make sure they
have a cold whatever-the-hell-he's-thirsty-for after his game. I
don't care what it takes, this is *rock and roll*, baby!"

After today's little stroll/expedition of walking around
peeking in, I make my way back to my office. A piece of
e-mail hits my in-box. Apparently, there's a special meeting
today in the serious conference room. Not the little Tuesday
marketing meeting conference room, the big one. The situation room, if you will. Where the entire company can be assembled to receive a message from Rush Hair and then see a
presentation from two guys that are supposed to be Internet
wunderkinds. The rumor is that the wunderkinds are going
to blow our minds. Have you ever had those days where you
think to yourself, "Nothing could blow my mind today; not a
perfect PowerPoint presentation, not Internet wunderkinds,
nothing." That's the way I'm feeling at the moment. In all fairness, sure, if one just started screaming like bad performance
artists, and running at us while screaming random jarring
phrases like "Christ-meat-stench-fist-rot!" and set one of the
conference-room chairs on fire and stared at it until he started
to weep, while the other wunderkind started running around
the conference room naked except for a rubber Nixon mask, a

couple of pieces of electrical tape on his nipples, and a fanny pack strapped to his chest filled with diet pills and a gun, and he was screaming something like, "Tiny radios live in my head and I want to eat my own heart!" — then, yeah, obviously, you know, mind-blowing. You'd be like, "Those guys really turned my head inside out with their presentation."

I get ready to leave my office and head to the conference room. The usual drill; quickly gather up enough gear to look responsible — my black binder/folder, *two* pens (*Awesome. Well done*), one of my fancy monogrammed notepads. As I leave my office and pass by Amy's desk, I let her know with a little bit of professional urgency why I'm heading right back out again:

"Just got an e-mail about the online music meeting, so I'm out again!" I raise my eyebrows with a what-are-you-gonna-do kind of face in hopes that I seem politely busy and super professional.

I grab a seat at the conference table just in time. These two enter the room in a sensible fashion. They set up their Power-Point. Rush Hair is already here. He gets up and tells the strangest story about how kids don't even go to record stores anymore, and how they're, get this, downloading music from the Internet these days. Rush Hair tells us that the problem with this is that it's killing the industry, because . . . well, partially because the biggest selection of online music resides on illegal networks where people get it for free since the legal options are still scant, to put it mildly. And even if people use the legal downloading option of the iTunes Music Store, it means they can download single tracks for a buck a pop, which basically means the industry can't sell a CD with only two or three good songs on it and get twenty bucks for it. I mean, this is never said out loud in our little family. I mean, maybe that kind of thing is said aloud in the upper reaches of the company, but down here it's all kind of one big elephant in the room.

"We are really excited about trying to figure out a way to sell albums online. This is a really exciting time. It's a challenging time, but it's an exciting time. And these gentlemen are here to give us a sneak preview of just how we might go about moving forward, " says Rush Hair.

He goes on to tell the story of how dangerous it is that kids are downloading from Limewire and these different peer-to-peer networks. He gives the example of coming home to find his daughters downloading music illegally on the Internet and seeing pornographic pictures on the same network. Note to self: apparently there is also free pornography on the peer-to-peer networks people use to illegally download music. *Dude. Seriously?*

"Can I please have everyone's attention?"

He tries to quiet the room so the Internet wunderkind twins can start their PowerPoint, but the idea of porn and music for free at the same time has created a buzz in the room. This must be what it felt like back in the heyday of the major record labels. People are chattering away, the electricity in the air feels like it just keeps flowing and flowing.

"Please. This is really exciting news, and I want to make sure everyone's listening before these gentlemen get started."

Sir, you might want to rethink your definition of exciting news after that little gem about free pornography that you opened with. He waits to get the room's attention. He looks at each person as if he's ready to say something again. I notice that this time I pay close attention. The room quiets down instantly. "Thank you. You need to give these gentlemen your undivided attention."

He notices how well this little eye-contact trick worked, and he raises his eyebrows kind of comically, adding, "See, that's why they pay me the big bucks. If you can do that, you can be president of a major record label and make a lot of money. *A lot* of money."

The joke doesn't really inspire laughter as much as it inspires people's faces to appear stunned at somebody finally admitting this aloud. I see a couple people looking at me. I panic for a moment, wondering if it's totally obvious that I'm sitting there thinking, *I wonder if I could make these people be quiet like that and make more money.*

The wunderkinds start their presentation. It's filled with very impressive color graphics that are broadcast from their laptops up onto the conference room's video screen. There are mocked-up frames of what this online music presence could look like, there are high-impact sights and sounds of the presentation, and then the whole idea basically boils down to people paying a monthly fee to have online access to a huge selection of the company's music, but only to listen to at their computers — not to actually download and have a copy of.

A few folks around the conference table pose a couple of respectably diligent devil's advocate questions, but it's clear that no praise is being handed out for that kind of thing, so that type of question quickly recedes. For the most part, we nod to indicate we understand and we nod more to seem like we find it all very interesting. It's important to look interested when you're told something is exciting. At the end of the presentation, we even do a little bit of clapping . . . you kind of have to, the way the presentation graphics zoom in and everything; you'd be kind of a jerk not to clap, really.

BLACK DOG

I walk into Vallerie's office a few days later; I need to talk to her about a new TV commercial that I'm going to be making for the Jewel album. She's on the phone but motions for me to stay, indicating that she'll be done in a moment, so while I wait I'm trying to be polite to Sylvia first. She's Vallerie's dog, and on Thursdays and Fridays little toy-size dogs like Sylvia are discreetly snuck into the building in designer handbags. Seems like a huge status-symbol thing with female executives here. One should know how to kind of schmooze the little dogs; it's actually an important protocol. Everyone here has it down. They have the sweet voice to talk to the dog with; they know what questions to ask and then how to make conversation with Vallerie based on the question they asked the dog. I have no idea how to talk to the tiny executive dogs when they're in the office. I grew up with big, dumb, friendly backyard dogs that made conversation easy. They would get happy when you came home from school. They'd look at you with a big smile, wagging their tail, and they seemed to be saying, "Throw my tennis ball! Throw it! Hey, throw my tennis ball! Throw! Throw it! Throw! Throw it, okay?" and you would just naturally say something like, "What are you doing? Does somebody want their tennis ball thrown? Is that what's going on here, mister?" and the dog would get really happy and start barking. But these tiny, smart, urbane dogs with designer stuff make me feel stupid for even saying anything to them at the office.

Sylvia's tucked away on her Burberry bed and doesn't seem to be saying anything, let alone wagging her tail because she's glad to see me, or asking to have a tennis ball thrown around. I don't really want to kneel down, so I just kind of aim my head toward the general direction of the Burberry bed and give talking to her my best shot.

"Is somebody in her big fancy office today?" I ask a little too loudly and matter-of-factly.

Out of the corner of my eye, I'm pretty sure I see Vallerie look up from her important phone call, and I realize the question was strangely and perfectly suited to her. Further confusing matters, I realize I asked the question in my regular voice, not a doggie voice. *Jesus, whisper, and do some kind of little doggie voice!* I step closer to the dog's designer bed in hopes of explaining my behavior a bit, and I whisper the question again.

"Is somebody staying in bed all day today, is that what's happening?" I ask in a rushed , loud whisper with a voice just slightly higher pitched than my natural voice. I am stunned to realize that I'm capable of sounding *exactly* like a middle-aged gay male nurse who's a little upset with a patient.

Still nothing from Sylvia. Either the dog doesn't consider her Burberry bed a "fancy office" and is pretty certain she's not going to "stay in bed all day," or she's just not in the mood for talking to me. *Jesus, dog. Cut me some slack here. Would it kill you to do something cute that'll make me look good in front of my boss?*

I put on a huge forced smile that seems odd to both me

and the dog, judging by the way it's shaking and quivering. I decide to go back to my normal voice. I try to think of what the hell to say.

Through my manic grin, I manage to whisper something like, "Well, hello there. Is it a good . . . day?"

Little Sylvia looks at me clearly nonplussed, totally silent, and does nothing. I stare at her and think, *Fine, dog. You can't say one little bark or run up to me? Two can play that fucking game, pal.*

I stand silently staring at it, saying not one word to it, and waiting for Vallerie to get off the phone.

Yeah, tough life for the executive dogs around here. Assistants take them for walks when they need to "do their business" — that is, unless they use a little pad on the floor. Working on the front lines of rock and roll is where I first heard the term *pee-pee pad*. Those are the little white quilted pads that some executives bring in with their little dogs, and they put one down in the corner of the office in case the dog needs to go out and the assistant's not around to take them out. Vallerie doesn't have one in her office, which I respect. But for one inspired second or two, I think about how cool it would be to get my own pee-pee pad and never have to leave my office to take a leak. Better still, I should make a power play for the top and get my own dog. But it's hard to imagine putting three thousand bucks on the table for something smaller than my shoe with a better pedigree than mine, so instead I stand waiting for Vallerie to get off the phone, and I'm daydreaming of what kind of office dog I would get. I think I'd head down to the pound and choose the cagiest, most high-strung, slouching, growling, medium-size passed-over derelict canine of the bunch. Something tortured by the dry itch of minor skin disorders to the point of lunacy. I would name him Taco. Taco would be too big to sneak in via handbag, so I would sneak him into the office on Thursdays and Fridays in a large duffle bag from the Army-Navy surplus store. I would have to wrestle the writhing duffle bag onto the elevator, occasionally coughing loudly in an attempt to cover up Taco's spasmodic, dry, hoarse growling.

Instead of a designer bed, Taco would prefer to sleep on a few flattened-out Kentucky Fried Chicken boxes that he'd licked clean of tasty grease. And when people would try to come into my office, Taco would freak out and start pulling on his chain, growling, barking, and bearing his aged gums and teeth like a deranged wolf fighting his way out of an errant bear trap. All the while, I'd be sitting there in my gray slacks and one of my sweaters or designer T-shirts saying in a really sensible voice with a smile, "Don't worry. You can put something on my desk, he's not going to bite you. He's just getting used to you."

As for a collar, Taco would have whatever was still hanging around his neck from the one person he let near him twelve years ago. And instead of trotting around the office and making a round of cute visits to everyone on the twenty-fourth floor, when Taco got off his chain, he would just be found in the employee kitchen chewing up a can of cleanser that he got from under the sink. And someone would have to call me to come get him because he'd have backed himself into a corner with his chewed-up cleanser can, freaking out in a low growl anytime anyone tried to come in and get some coffee, because he'd think they were trying to take his cleanser away.

"Hi. Jewel spot." She says after hanging up.

I try one last shot at this. "I was just saying hello to your little helper."

Vallerie looks over at her, doesn't even say a word, and Sylvia comes alive and starts doing little barks and cute little running around. Sylvia looks at me like she knows exactly what she's doing. *What the hell do you have against me, dog?*

"Uh, right," I say, "the Jewel commercial."

Vallerie starts to look at papers on her desk, the dog continues showing respect by doing cute things even though Vallerie's not even watching. I sort of squint at the dog like a bitter middle child.

Still looking down at her papers and gathering the details, Vallerie gives me the lowdown, "We need a sixty, and also a fifty-five with a blank five-second back end that we can use to tag with sponsors. And you should use 'Intuition' because that's going to be the first single. And it looks like we should have the finished video in-house by tomorrow."

Easy enough. What could possibly throw a wrench into that? I make a polite exit from Vallerie's office, straddling my way over the little makeshift doggie gate at her door. Behind me, the sound of a happy little dog playing it up for Vallerie, Senior Vice President of Marketing. I feel like it's going to tell her to fire me.

THE SOUND OF UNSETTLING

I walk back into my office and there's this little story in each trade magazine that has been laid on my desk. Someone may be buying the company. Bear in mind that this rumor has been floating around for years. There was even a close call with EMI buying this place along with the other labels that fall under the umbrella of the Warner Music Group, but the deal went south. So, it's not out of the normal range of gossip to hear about rumors that our parent company has still got Warner Music Group on the block. We're still owned by Time Warner at the moment, but the new twist to the rumor of the sale is this: the billionaire grandson of a man who made the family a fortune in booze and industrial chemical dealings might buy this place. Not a bad twist, really. In Hollywood terms I'd say a billionaire grandson with an inheritance is right up there with a great white shark bent on evening the score with humans, or a spirit that refuses to move on to the afterlife. Certainly gets one's attention at the end of a long day. There's a lot to feel insecure about if you work in the record business in this digital age, but what are you gonna do? Personally, I choose to continue doing my work while people way smarter and higher up the ladder hopefully figure it all out. And I deal with the feelings the responsible, adult way: I use Starbucks baked goods to shove the feelings way down into my stomach. Then I pour something called caramel machiatto on them so they can't come back to life, and then it's time to start writing

the script to the Jewel commercial. Then if the script gets approved, I'll check in to an editing studio across town and start
cutting footage from her videos into a commercial. But the
script isn't going anywhere. It's already been a long day; so the
first pass has some problems.

JEWEL SCRIPT, TV 0:60, FIRST DRAFT

Open on shot of Jewel from "Intuition" video where she's
crossing the street and looking beautiful in evening dress with
small handbag, laughing. *Why is she laughing? It's kind of odd,
really, isn't it? To just cross the street by yourself all dolled up
and laughing, laughing, laughing. It's like a crazy person. That's
my favorite kind of crazy person; the ones that are just cracking
up, holding something random like a can of frosting and laughing their ass off at you while you walk by. Okay, focus. Let's do
this.* After she gets across street, graphic elements from album
cover fade up in cross walk, almost like wherever she steps, she
leaves an imprint that is a cool graphic.

VOICEOVER

Are you ready for a revolution? *Holy Christ, reel it in. This is
not a revolution.* Are you ready for a new . . . uh . . . CD? *Okay,
wait . . . here:*

VOICEOVER

Jewel. *0304.* The new album. A whole new sound that . . .
might . . . save us? Since we are trapped here waiting to be
fired in a massive bloodletting. And I'm afraid I've become
accustomed to the lifestyle of middle management. Please . . .
buy the album so I don't have to face the realities of life and

I can continue to eat something called a blueberry bliss bar with something called a caramel macchiato, maintaining a total denial of my days slipping by in this finite life. Okay, it's late. It's been a long day and I'm going home. Jewel. *0304*. The new album . . . in stores now. Good night.

Vallerie stops by first thing to say "good morning" with a huge smile on her face. She's looking at me with eyes that seem to strike that very familiar chord; a chord that you know the second you see it if you grew up with an older sibling. The kind that lies somewhere between kindness, terror, and killing boredom with comedic pastime. She announces a little piece of news the way my sister would announce something like this, as if the choice was between laughing so hard you start crying, and simply talking it through and trying to pull it off so that she could die laughing later.

"Okay, the president of our parent company, AOL – Time Warner" — pauses. Gets it together — "has invited a young lady here from China — because, as you know, AOL has all these ideas about making inroads into China — anyway" — again, hand goes up to eye to wipe away what might be hint of a tear — "Okay, anyway, she's coming to visit for a week and guess who I told him she should spend three days with while she's here!"

"Oh, classic. Awesome. Is she going to hang out with the guy from . . ."

"*You!*"

And then she starts cracking up and at the same time sort of moves closer to me, grabbing my arm in a cross between a gesture designed to comfort me and an effective move to keep me from running. It's at this moment I realize she knows something. That maybe there's some truth to the new sale rumor. Here's what I think:

1. That after twenty years of working here, and with the threat of mergers hanging over the company during the last two or three years recently refreshed by the rumor of the grandchild of the liquor czar buying this place, and fueled by yet another year of decreased sales, she realizes what is happening to this business.

2. This devilishly euphoric prankster standing in my office is proof that Vallerie has clearly decided that she's not sticking around. I sit there watching her laugh; smile, eyes, teeth, lips, this is it. I've felt this feeling a million times before looking at a smile, eyes, teeth, and lips — she is someone about to be gone.

There's an almost terrifying sense of freedom that comes to somebody who has faced a very finite truth. And it's a sense of freedom that scares the hell out of those of us who haven't had the guts to face a very finite truth yet. Those of us who are still running from it; those of us who are hoping that whatever job we're working at every day of our lives is going to add up to something far brighter than we could ever imagine, even though every single solitary sublime sign and cue points to the exact opposite being true. Yeah, well, good for her. Because none of this changes the fact that somewhere in Shanghai some Chinese chick is packing a suitcase and coming to America to be my shadow.

———————

Christina arrives. Christina. All the way from Shanghai, and her name is Christina? This is already shaping up wrong.

Maybe that's just her "American" name. Dashed are my day-dreams of introducing my new friend Huan Lin Yao to my pedestrian peers with boring everyday names like Steve.

Christina . . . Who does she think she's fooling with her little impromptu hotel and airport alias, I think to myself, for some reason in the voice of that woman on the old television show called *Murder, She Wrote.*

Jesus, I realize in about four seconds that I know nothing about China. I should've at least read up on it on the Internet or something right before she got here. At least I'd be able to impress her by having done some kind of homework. "Hi there, *Christina,* it's sure nice to have a visitor from Shanghai, the city of 6,341 square kilometers with a population of thir-teen million. You guys on track to get that twelve to fourteen inches of average annual precipitation? Still got the Brown-Eared Pheasant as the national bird over there? Or is your province's bird the Crested Ibis? It may well be, come to think of it. Well, as the Chinese proverb says, 'Nothing stands out like a crane amongst a flock of chickens.' Ah, ha ha ha ha . . . yes . . . well . . ." But instead I quietly and kindly offer her a seat when she shows up in my office. Amy brings in a couple bottles of water for us.

"Are you guys set, do you need anything?"

"Yeah, no. Thanks. I don't think, I mean, water is prob-ably . . . good," I answer.

"This is great. It's an interesting time for you to be here checking things out. If you guys want to order lunch or need anything, let me know," Amy offers.

Christina smiles. Amy leaves. We enjoy about a minute and half of silence while we are simply enjoying the terror of the silence while smiling politely at each other.

Then I figure the best thing to do, evidently, is to spasm into a diatribe about 1979 Los Angeles punk, and how when I was little I woke up one night, walked into the living room, and the eleven-o'clock news was doing a story on the band X, playing at the Universal amphitheater.

Turns out that the nice thing about spontaneous fits of awkward expository monologues from a man sixteen years older than Christina is that they sometimes break the ice. She and I start talking about favorite bands and albums, college radio, and underground pirate radio stations. She's really cool! She tells me all about the pirate radio show in Shanghai that she hosts with her boyfriend. And she's wearing these really cool Chinese knock-offs of Converse high-tops. I tell her they're cool and she explains that they can't get real Converse in China. I ask her if it's because the government won't allow it. No, not really, it turns out — just hard to get and too expensive there. I find that aside from comparing notes on new bands and old favorites, my only persistent contribution from my end are questions about government oppression. She tells me her boyfriend can't keep doing the radio show (*Fascists cracking down on you over there?*) because he feels he has gotten behind in his studies at school. That she's only staying here for five days (*Commies got you on a tight leash, do they?*) because she would like to visit friends in Utah. She tells me that even though piracy runs rampant in China, they still have all of these great underground record stores in Shanghai, where you can buy music from bands that aren't the huge worldwide hits getting bootlegged and sold on the street corners.

"Underground, as in 'we need to hide it so the fascists don't crush it? So they won't take it from us?'"

"What?"

"Nothing."

The next two days of her visit are spent mostly at the editing studio, where I am working on the Jewel commercial. And Christina loves it there. I love it there, too. The contrast between the offices and the editing studio, where my friend Ben works, is night and day. You walk around there unafraid of corporate protocol and the weight of who you say and don't say hello to when you pass through the halls. There's laughter and very loud music to trade comments on, jokes to tell, and weekend stories — all of the things you don't find back at the offices.

While Christina is around, we're watching footage from the Jewel video together on two big editing screens, cutting it down to make a rough version of the TV commercial for her new record. There's a point when Christina asks if this new look and sound is supposed to be a reinvention for Jewel. Having now written and revised the script for the commercial countless times, after endless input from Dick and management, finally arriving at the perfect line (turns out that "the new album *0304* is an *exciting* step in the *breathtaking* career of Jewel") — which will let North America know just how big this reinvention is — I tell Christina that yes, it is indeed a reinvention of some kind. She asks me if I think it seems sincere, this reinvention, or more like a gimmick. I tell her I've heard that the whole thing's supposed to be somehow ironic, and I say that it seems a little gimmicky to me, but that it's not my job to say that. I say I think it probably started out as a sort of satire of selling out, but that too many people got involved and next thing you know, it wasn't coming across like irony or satire, but it's not my job to say things like this. I can think stuff like that, but I gotta hide those thoughts from the Man.

What am I saying this for? I could get in trouble. I could get fired. I say something about how Jewel and her reinvention will probably succeed wildly in alienating her faithful fans, maybe winning a few thousand fair-weather friends that won't be around for the next album.

Dude! Hello? Take it back! I backpedal like crazy. I consider the political implications of telling an intern invited by the CEO of our parent company what I think about all this. I cover my ass and I say that, to Jewel's credit, maybe she's making the most integral move she can imagine making as an artist and probably doesn't care if this record sells less, because she's doing whatever she wants to do and that's what being an artist is all about.

And there you go, there's my little reinvention of *my* own sound. Christina looks at me like she has just seen her first real tourist attraction in America: a little tiny record businessman totally afraid to say what he thinks about a record. *Oh, come on, sister . . . you're from Communist China. I shouldn't have to tell you that it's all about saying the right thing when you know it could get back to the wrong people.*

We continue cutting and recutting. Scene by scene from the big-budget video is cut down, frame by frame, into our little commercial. Ben moves the footage on screen forward and backward, forward and backward, looking for points to make his cuts in perfect time. Christina and I sit on the studio's big couch and watch the monitors. A pretty girl, who became a pop star, moves forward across the street very quickly, then backward slowly, then forward again, and on and on until a

cut is made into the next scene and then the new scene starts
the same back-and-forth drill. Repeat for the next four hours,
and then it's time to head back to the office. On our walk
Christina tells me that the editing studios are more like what
she thought the record company offices would be like.

We pass through the revolving doors just in time for Vallerie
to see us. She comes over to say hello.

"Oh, my God, there you are! I think she has a crush on
you! What was it like, was it weird! Oh, God, I saw you two
walking around. I started laughing so hard I had to duck into
Lee's office and set down my coffee so I didn't spill it all over
myself!"

Okay, this conversation is clearly not intended for our guest's
ears. And two seconds ago, as far as I can recall, Christina
was standing right next to me. She's short, but still, I mean,
she's standing right here. Maybe Vallerie thinks there's a
language barrier? I try to give indication — by way of odd
combinations of subtly nodding my head and raising my eyebrows — that the intern is very near the two of us. I try feebly
to steer the conversation toward the weather or lunch or just
about anything else besides how funny Vallerie seems to think
it is that Christina and I are spending three days together and
that we seem inseparable.

"Do you . . . is . . . um . . ." I stammer before she interrupts
me again, happy as hell to keep going on.

"And you still have two days left! Oh, God, it's just too
funny! This is so classic. Okay . . . so, what's she like? What do
you two even talk about!"

I cough loudly. "Okaaaaay, so, looks like rain out there.
Anytime now. Going to lunch? I What do you think you'll

have today, for lunch? Do you like the rain, having lived in London?"

Vallerie looks at me as if I've just erupted into the type of brief monologue usually associated with the clinically insane. I look down at my right side where I last saw Christina and realize she's not there. I whip my head around to my left side to see if she's there. She is not. This leaves one option: that is, that she has disappeared around the back of me. Maybe she's right up against me? [She can be shy if she doesn't know you, so] maybe she's hiding. Vallerie excuses what appears to be my mildly psychotic episode and goes on.

"Well, I think she's cute! I think you two make" — starts her laughing thing where she won't be able to stop — "Oh, my God . . . seeing you" — more laughing, this is getting so dangerous that I'm grinding teeth the happier she gets — "you two make such a weird perfect pair to be running around midtown Manhattan together!" — laughing again — "Like! . . . Like some kind of strange movie about a duo who . . ."

Suddenly Vallerie looks down at my left side. Stunned silence. Guess who came into view.

Christina beams and adds a little wave: "Hi!"

To which Vallerie replies, "Oh! Well . . . Hello!"

And I add, "Okay, so . . . lunch for you." And with that we part ways, Christina and I heading to the elevator. Upstairs, I leave a videocassette of the rough cut on Vallerie's desk so she can check it out when she gets back.

LIMERICK
COUNTY LIBRARY

Do the Evolution:
Ideas for Two Other Possible Ironic
Image Reinventions

1. Jewel Reinvented: Heavy Metal Jewel!

Come up with satanic acronym for J.E.W.E.L. (Jesus Eats What Everyone Loves? Not so good, but will work on this, you guys.)

Invent new angle on back story: Yes, she lived in a van in the early days. That's because it was easier to *worship Satan* without having to worry about tipping off neighbors, etc. Yodeling? *Speaking in tongues!* If you were one of the Knights in Jewel's Service (new name for fan club?), you would have understood the message.

Art direction: Hair? Black. Guitar? Black. The standard blue-jeans you're used to seeing her in? More like *black* jeans.

Leak rumors to press:

- White doves were going to be used in the new video . . . that is, until J.E.W.E.L. tore them into pieces and threw the bloodied bird carcasses out into a crowd of shocked, frightened onlookers on set.
- Play "Who Will Save Your Soul?" backward and the answer to the musical question is a revealed when you hear the back-masked phrases "Satan will save," "Dark Lord, he will save it," and "Sing for me, children of Satan, I am Alaskan."
- Allowed editors to use her actual blood in red ink for the Jewel Comic Book and Jewel Army Newsletter.
- Prays to devil before each concert.

2. Hootie and the Blowfish Repackaged: Hardcore Gangster Rap!

First thing: Front man Darius Rucker to dis other rappers in press, should be timed to the release of a newly remixed, remastered box set of their hits called *Straight outta Columbia, South Carolina* in reference to N.W.A's seminal *Straight Outta Compton*.

Shorten name to "Ho Blow"?

New video for remake of "Hold My Hand" now called "Hold My Handgun" and will be the only "new" track on *Straight out of Columbia, South Carolina* box set.

Shoot video in same house where they filmed the "Let Her Cry" video in 1994, but now it's well over a decade later, the place is littered with old vials and glass pipes, stained with the vaguely antiestablishment, crack-fueled graffiti of aimless addicts. Windows are boarded up.

Drummer plays with his shirt off whole time, just like in original, but now we see his "bullet wounds" (latex/makeup) where he was "shot *ten* times" — that's one more than 50 Cent clamed fyi — "at point-blank range, but managed to survive and foster a reputation as hardest, baddest, blah, blah, blah."

Hire freelance writer to pen badass investigative piece entitled "Where was Darius on the night Tupac was shot?" Piece could posit "theory" that Darius and guitarist Mark Bryan were both unaccounted for in the lineup of obvious suspects. Best-case scenario, it reopens the case in the public eye and gets the Columbia, South Carolina, region included in on East Coast–West Coast hip-hop feuds of nineties, garnering the band some street cred.

The Salvation of Stooges

It's a few weeks later, well after Christina has left the corridors of corporate rock for the wide-open spaces of Utah. The end of another day, and Ben and I are heading out from the editing studio to meet up with his brother Nat at a diner in Times Square to get something to eat. Some tourist place on Broadway with singing waitresses, a smattering of tourists, and three now gainfully employed men, living well inside the law and meeting up for something to eat after work. We take turns complaining about office politics or the workload in our respective places of business. I'm chain-sipping Diet Coke so fast that our singing waitress automatically brings a refill without missing a beat of "Summer Lovin'" from *Grease* and just before she launches into Sinatra's trademark "New York, New York," which I have to admit takes on a certain poetic undertone when sung by a twenty-six-year-old from the Midwest carrying a basket of cheese fries and a Diet Coke. I pull my head off the straw long enough to think these thoughts in caffeinated succession:

- Odd place for grown men to have dinner after work.
- I would not have guessed I'd wind up like this, a thirty-five-year-old desk-job guy trying not to check out a twenty-six-year-old singing waitress.

But then I remember why were here in the first place: we're going to see Iggy and the Stooges! I don't think it has hit any of us yet that we're going to see Iggy Pop after dinner, but before long we're walking up Broadway to Roseland, and it's hard not to notice that the pace is one of those paces you recall from when you were maybe seventeen and a brand-new Friday night was unfolding in front of you and you don't want to miss a thing.

We walk into Roseland and there's some terrible situation onstage: Godsmack? I don't know much about this band. I guess, really, I know nothing about this band, but evidently they seem to be a pop metal band of men doing an acoustic unplugged set and singing about their feelings, which is fine and everything and they're probably great guys and everything, but frankly tonight we're confused as to why they're here. Hell, *they're* probably confused as to why they're here, in all fairness. Some guy introducing them keeps saying that he's the new host of the all-new *Headbanger's Ball* on MTV2 and nobody in the crowd seems to know why this is important. And I figure that maybe we should split while we can, wait outside for Iggy to go on, before the shouting MTV2 host and his network promotional skills snuffs the excitement we've felt up to this point.

The guys onstage tune up their acoustic guitars and start another song about emotions and all I'm thinking about are the record executives at work and how they would probably think that somebody was brilliant to put these guys on before Iggy with nothing but acoustic guitars. They would probably say it's "Exposing them to a crossover demographic that may have missed them the first time around in the nineties" and then they'd start into, like, almost a seizure where they're regurgitating two or three dozen marketing maxims at a time about how it made sense for this band to open. It's terrible to be standing here subjected to the bad marketing and promotion initiatives of middle-aged rich white men in high-rises when you came here for something that rails against that very kind of thing. You came here for Iggy Pop, the last bastion of hope against that kind of thinking and selling. And then something happens that reaffirms faith: I look around and notice that most of the crowd have simply elected to either read a book or hang out and talk in groups of three or four. Then in between songs and MTV announcements, folks near where we're standing simply hold their middle fingers aloft without taking their eyes off their book or conversation they're having. Oh, sweet, sweet New York, how I love you so. Then the MTV guy comes out once more talking again about how he's the host of the all-new *Headbanger's Ball* on MTV2, and how we all have to tune in. The crowd is a mix of laughter, some booing, and another round of middle fingers held high. There is hope! Stagehands eventually start breaking down equipment and moving new guitars out and tuning them. The unplugged so-called alternative metal songs have stopped being played, and the opening band has retreated, maybe even a little earlier than they planned, making me think they're probably decent men on some level. After about twenty minutes, the house lights go down, the stage goes dark, some static and clamor as a guitar is plugged in by a shadowy figure, static for a second, a little feedback, and then the first huge chords ring out and . . .

JEEEEZUS!

The stage lights are up full blast and Iggy Pop hits the stage like he's not going to stop running until he's at the back of the auditorium, grabs the mic, and splits off across the stage to the side. A shirtless blur, a tornado of living, screaming, chiseled muscle-and-sinew proof that all of what they told you about growing up or aging is bullshit.

Mike Watt, from the Minutemen and fIREHOSE, is playing bass and looks as amazed as anyone in the crowd. His eyes are absolutely glued to Iggy, and Iggy is everywhere at once. He flies like a computer-animated god-beast deity in an unhinged and hijacked Lucas film. You suddenly realize every punk band you thought was blowing your mind back when you were sixteen was simply a cute little messenger delivering a wadded note to you from this man, wherever he might have been that night. In retrospect, the punk shows you went to when you were growing up all seem like long-distance calls on a speakerphone from a place only somewhat near the storm you're witnessing firsthand now.

Ron Asheton plays guitar like he's seen it all before, but the rest of us . . . Jesus! Iggy has sprinted across the stage for the eighth time since a minute ago and, in the blink of an eye, with one simple jump and a lightning-fast pull-up, this fifty-six-year-old life force has launched his frame up onto an eight-foot stack of amp cabinets. He stands up on top and is on the mic again in a flash, face-to-face with the industry suits up in the balcony at the side of the stage. "Betcha wish you weren't fat!" he wails at them, like a perfect storm of wiseass howl, fire, and cat-call taunt. He's singing like his life depends on it, even more than any frontman thirty years younger than he is; like he knows it's been a could-end-any-minute ride since he was seventeen and he wants to have one last laugh at those who chose the safe and staid path just in case tonight's the last time he gets to show them what life is like when you're living it. "Jump down here you fat fucks! I dare you to jump! You won't jump because you're scared!" all of this grin-and-scream lasting about three and one-eighth seconds before he's airborne back down to the stage. I stand slack-jawed on the verge of crying like one of those girls in the black-and-white footage of the Beatles on *Ed Sullivan*. Iggy Pop is screaming, writhing, running, grinning, howling, singing, posing like a man-god returned from the volcano, and then lurching back into a tornado of fuel and fever and guess-what-I've-been-up-here-since-before-your-heroes-were-born-and-they-said-it-wouldn't-last-another-minute-in-1976-fuckers!

The experience is nearing religious if you're one of the legions who have spent a lifetime so far rudderless. I am trying to reason, the way you maybe try to reason when a UFO is coming down in front of the family station wagon on Interstate 10 somewhere just outside of New Mexico or wherever they land. Try to figure out how you're seeing what you're seeing, but for Christ's sake, don't miss a detail. The Da Vinci drawing with the punk rock head on top of it, every muscle impossibly etched, is now swinging the microphone over his head by its cable, in maybe a fifteen-foot circle. Guitarist casually ducks it, Watt plays his bass backing up a bit, still looking as awestruck as the rest of us. Doesn't even look out to the crowd until about the fifth song and even then it feels as if he's just looking to make sure there are going to be other witnesses. Iggy is screaming for everybody to come up on stage! Um, unfortunately, Mr. Pop, I am paralyzed and almost crying like a goddamned housewife in the front row of Tom Jones at Caesar's Palace, so I'm not gonna be able to get up there with the others. Suddenly maybe two hundred people are climbing over the barricade and crashing security, who resist the flood at first, then decide quickly to step aside as Iggy, still hitting every lyric, manages between lines and breaths to scream things like, "Don't fucking listen to them! I said get up onstage! It's my fucking show and you're the one who paid! Get up here! Have fun, goddammit!"

The stage fills up fast, Iggy disappears into the mass, invisible with his anti-status-quo wrath but still making sure you hear every word at nine million decibels plus whatever the mic and sound system add to it. And you fight to explain all of this in your head, this feeling that you're witnessing something biblical in an age not known for miracles. Your brain races to explain it before giving in to the music again. You tell yourself he is simply controlled by dead Indians, like Ouija boards and fortune-tellers. You apologize inside for every single solitary moment of life you have ever wasted sitting still.

Iggy Pop continues at the exact same level of intensity that he sprinted to the stage with for what has added up to at least two solid hours, and then he screams goodnight, contorts his body into a combination of major-league fastball windup and yoga stretch, then tilts focus totally downward, and releases the pitch, hurling the microphone down with all his strength, straight into the stage. As the smash of the mic's high-speed encounter with the stage still rings in the speakers, the Stooges continue to play the song out. Iggy Pop is walking offstage and something starts going crazy down left in the crowd. A fight? A knife? What? Wait! In another split-second blur, it becomes clear that Iggy Pop is making his way through the crowd with the weird, unexplained, and improbable speed of some kind of snake you've heard about humans not being able to outrun. The only evidence of his path is a parting wake of fans that cuts and zags a sudden swath, with outfoxed secu-

rity guys trailing behind, and within about three seconds flat
you see Iggy Pop *scaling the wall up to the VIP mezzanine!* A
long rope of sinewy muscle with hair and eyes on top, Iggy
hangs from the ledge with the fastest of the huge security guys
hanging on to his foot — but Iggy wriggles it free in the blink
of an eye and pulls himself quickly up above the crowd. In
what feels like less than five seconds he has flown from the
stage to the ledge of the auditorium's mezzanine. The idle rich
hipsters and industry VIP crowd up there are shocked and
wide-eyed with *"Holy shit, the gargoyle flew up here! Hold on
to your complimentary Skyy vodka and cranberry, you guys!"*
written on their faces.

Iggy runs the length of the elevated former safe harbor of
the privileged, turning over tables, heaving them up and over
and grinning maniacally, explosions of sprayed and flung al-
cohol flagging his eastbound advance through them. Chairs
are flying, tables are sailing over, he moves fast with almost
casual fury in this ultimately harmless but overdue, inspired,
urgent, and precision reconnaissance mission. And as quickly
as he came, he is gone, and the well-dressed and shocked
stand amongst the debris looking at each other and down
at their clothes covered in champagne or booze mixed with
juice. He reappears at the edge of the mezzanine, jumps back
down into the crowd, cuts and swerves invisibly and springs
back on stage, screaming his final good-byes two hours after
this all started. And this time when he leaves, the band wraps
up the song, walks off, and the house lights are up fast like
nothing ever happened. Like the authorities are telling you it
couldn't have been a UFO that crushed your station wagon's
hood when you found yourself blinded and transported, then
set back down with an unexplained lapse of two hours.

Every single one of us makes our way to the doors dazed and calm while a tiny digital facsimile of music from a CD plays through the house speakers. We are a mass of people maybe finally repaired, just back from our Lourdes, borne through wide double doors and out into the night of Times Square, and it feels like every single excuse you were ever planning to use has been stripped away by what you just saw happen. Like you're going out into the world to try again, apologizing to God and yourself for any moment of blood coursing through your veins that you ever took for granted.

On the way home we walk east and pass by the office. I stand there at the base of the building looking up and thinking, I go there every day and sit in one square of that glass grid and I keep my mouth shut in meetings. I count the stories up to twenty-four and try to figure out exactly which office is mine. Ben says that the way the building is flanked by two shorter buildings one could argue that it looks like a middle finger extended, and therefore spending all day there could essentially pass for a rebellious gesture. Ben is laughing at the thought of this. I think I see the tiny square where I sit way up off the street.

After good-bye, Ben heads downtown, and I split to the F subway through the plaza at Rockefeller Center where they're setting up for MTV Video Music Awards, which happen tomorrow night. It's maybe one-thirty in the morning and the red carpet is already rolled out and lit by eighteen million watts of halogen, even though there's nobody on it. They have already barricaded two long paparazzi pits that run up either side, the entire length of it — from Fifth Avenue, through the plaza, and into a celebrity entrance covered by white tents. I walk down the red carpet very uncelebrated, toward my usual

shortcut to the subway on Forty-ninth, while a night watch-
man sits at the edge of the carpet reading a newspaper, watching nothing. Tomorrow this well-lit ghost town will come
alive — a petri dish of lip-synch teen sensations arriving with
moms for managers, moguls for agents, and silently stewing
best friends for personal assistants; a bright red, fifty-yard,
narrow, fecund swamp of pop flavors of the month, diamond-
encrusted hip-hop braggarts with bejeweled hangers-on, and
cute boys who decided to play pop-punk instead of model or
star in a sitcom. I walk along the carpet, hands in my pockets,
Iggy Pop forever screaming in my head.

Ladies and Gentlemen, Please Put Your Hands Together for "Middle-Aged Billionaire and the Prestigious Investors"!

Fact: You can be a grown man and be worrying about having your job yanked up and out of your hands by some guy's grandson who's got it in his head he wants to buy himself a music company. This is so sadly funny to me — that you can wind up in this position as an adult.

I keep thinking of him as a cross between Mr. Burns from *The Simpsons* and a giant infant monster running amok in sort of herky-jerky motion against a skyline, like some kind of sixties sci-fi Ray Harryhausen stop-motion animation. I literally have to make an effort to remember he's a grown man. We're so clearly doomed. Morale is unbelievably low.

There are these e-mails that have started floating around. Nobody's getting fired yet, the deal hasn't even gone through, but the few guys on the twenty-eighth floor are cleaning house and giving some people "the option" to leave. Probably in hopes of making numbers look a little better and saving their own ass when this guy becomes our new stepdad. These sudden dispatches — creepy, strained corporate good-byes/eulogies from people who have suddenly decided that "There is an opportunity to move on and explore other things in life after ten great years . . ." — are showing up almost daily in our in-boxes. They feel as if they're typed at gunpoint. Like you should be reading them for prearranged, secret phrases or clues that would convey a message of whereabouts or safety. "I've decided it's time to move on." You bet; makes perfect sense when you think about it. The economy is the weakest it's been in the last twelve years, unemployment is at a ten-year high, the cost of living in New York has remained staggering and unadjusted to the current recession. It just makes good sense that it's time to take the leap into opening that home-based salsa and sauces business that your friends said you should start when they tasted your pasta sauce at your dinner party a year ago.

You can only imagine what went on behind closed doors to generate these little flurries of faked and steely optimism laced with supposed midlife desires to open a small business or spend more time on hobbies and travel. And they're always followed by a note from the two or three guys making millions and still running this show. "There are some changes going on, and I wanted to communicate them to you so that you understand that . . . everything . . . is . . . fine. I repeat: Bob from sales was not harmed. He is very happy to be moving on, and he said that in an e-mail today. Please continue to go about your work. We are a big family. Continue to work. *Faaaaammmmily.*"

THE BENDS

Vallerie has just come into my office crying. Apparently the guys upstairs are hauling people in and giving them the option between a 50 percent salary cut or a severance package. She's sitting in my office stunned and shaken, not believing twenty years would end this way, when an e-mail from the guys upstairs about how she's "decided to move on and will be missed" hits my in-box. And the end of the e-mail celebrates Ms. Chocolate Chip being promoted into Vallerie's position as Senior Vice President of Marketing — head of the marketing department and my direct boss as of about five minutes ago. Look, I know I'm marred with a good old-fashioned alcoholic lust for career suicide, and I know by now you've figured out that I'm a pessimist hardwired to fail, just like any other semitalented malcontent burdened by self-absorption, minor chemical imbalance, and the guilt of wasting years, but you have to admit that this is shaping up to look like the end.

I read in the *Wall Street Journal* this morning that some of our top brass are expected to "exit" as early as this week. They specifically cited Rush Hair as being most likely one of the first to go.

There's this weird calm and tension around here today. Assistants speak in urgent hushed whispers and dart about from office to office like birds who can sense the storm approaching. They're trying to make good impressions on everyone — not just the people they assist — because who knows who'll be left to work for. At first this confuses me and I think every attractive young woman in her early twenties working on this floor has developed a sudden interest in me. Vallerie leaves my office, and for the next half hour it seems like every time I look up from my computer, there's another assistant sitting in the chair in front of my desk asking to speak with me. I look up once and a young brunette girl that I recognize as an assistant to Aging Suburban Rocker Guy is sitting there.

"I've always wanted to just work with music. You know? That's all I've ever wanted to do my whole life, really. You've been a big influence on me in this business [?] and I just want to say that I appreciate that."

"O . . . kay. Hello."

Cut to another attractive young woman that I recognize from walking by her cubicle every day for the last year and a half.

"No matter what happens around here, I just want to say that it's been really cool. I grew up so far from all of this. In the country! Out in the sticks! But I love New York. I really do, I love it here. And I love the record business. I like the . . . the . . . marketing? That you've done."

It all feels like a completely inappropriate kind of speed-dating event.

She continues, "If you need help with anything, let me know. I can help you do whatever."

"Okay, well . . . I like working here. With you. Working here together."

And then a male assistant.

"Hey, man. I just want to say whatever happens around here with all the changes, you've really been an inspiration. I really hope our paths cross in this business again. You're definitely the kind of guy I'd like to be in this business when I'm your age."

"Uh, I'm only . . ."

Amy comes into my office and the young man I've inspired leaves. She tells me she's given her notice and is moving into a management position at a magazine across town. Maybe the smartest move anyone in the building has really made in the time I've been here.

I still can't believe the situation with Chocolate Chip; yesterday she was still a video producer; she was still the person to call if you were a pop star demanding a midget in the dream sequence of your music video, or if you've figured out that what you need is a high-class hooker pretending to be the stewardess on the rented private jet you're doing your photo shoot on. But now she's moving into Vallerie's corner office as soon as it's cleared out.

If a scuba diver attempted an ascent as suddenly, it would result in the bends — eyeballs bulging free of ocular cavities, and a lifetime of amnesia and babbling insanity — but this week in our little family, something like this is called good old-fashioned upward mobility.

WELCOME TO THE NEW
MARKETING MEETING, BABY

It's Tuesday morning, and I'm on the uptown 9 train because — as I keep telling myself over and over in a silent mantra — never leaving the apartment and living the rest of my thirties without expectations and in a delightfully aimless trance of cable television and junk food only *sounds* like a good idea. This is the first Tuesday-morning marketing meeting that Vallerie will have no part in. It is, in fact, in the hands of Ms. Chocolate Chip herself, since she is the new head of the department.

I get off at Rockefeller Center, walk up Sixth Avenue, and enter the revolving doors at 1290 to catch the elevator going up. Off the elevator, past the frosted glass doors, and through the lobby. I see that there's now a small, lit-up sign hung in the lobby that simply states how many records have been sold by this guy who works on the twenty-third floor and has his own in-house label here. Been here for twenty years, and he's really the only guy in the building who has consistently signed hit acts and sold massive records in the last few years. The company set him up with his own label, then after another string of hits he sold it to them for anywhere from $12–40 million, depending on whom you talk to. He or one of his employees has invested in a sign that allows you to customize a scrolling

message like LV RECORDS. . . . OVER 80 MILLION RECORDS SOLD
WORLDWIDE and has hung it in the lobby. I think two things:

1. Genius.
2. He's made that much money for the company and he's
   worried about defending himself in the event of a sale
   and merger? I'm screwed.

Okay, down the hall, late, damn it, late, Jesus, late, why, late.
I speed-walk into my office to gear up: notepad, pen, and also
highlighter pen (*brilliant*), I grab my black plastic binder as well.
*Dude, what else, a stapler? A three-hole punch? Just get going,
you're late.* I run out hoping I'm carrying enough responsible-
looking office supplies to offset the fact that I am at least fifteen minutes (*damn, fine, twenty, twenty, twenty, shut up,
just walk — faster*) late for this meeting. Down the hall to the
conference room. Pause a second so the door isn't hammered
open with a speed-walker shoulder-check. One deep breath,
and I open the door.

Look at this, the meeting is in full swing. I walk in. She's
staring right at me. I think. Her head is pointed at me, anyway,
but it's hard to tell if her eyes are focusing on me since she's . . .
sweet moses . . . she's wearing *sunglasses*. In the office. It's not
even bright in here. It's not even bright *outside* today. She looks
up over them to make it clear she has noted my coming in late.
I'm trying to see if there's an open seat somewhere along the
conference table, but I keep staring back as I walk. *Yes. Sunglasses. Are you sure? Look again. Yes. Sunglasses. Okay, quit
it, quit looking.* I can't take my eyes off the situation, though!
She's not talking. Nobody's talking, really, and I'm not sure
if that's because I've entered late or if I've come in during a

lull. There's some minor perspiration under my hair from all of my speed-walking, and as I make my way toward an open seat, I am rewarded with a refreshing cool feeling on my scalp, which, to my surprise, makes me smile pleasantly. I'm afraid the blissful smile, coupled with my double take, is making me come off as bemused with the idea of our new leader wearing sunglasses in the marketing meeting. Several of the younger assistants and foot soldiers seated around the table take note of my expression and start grinning themselves. There's no way now for me to explain to them that I'm simply refreshed by the cooling sensation on my scalp, so I just nod hello to them and sit down. She resumes.

"Okay, well we've got a rough cut of Ryan Cabrera's video in. So, if someone will turn off the lights, we'll take a look at that. It's really cool."

Someone obliges on the lights, rendering our new leader blind, one would have to presume.

The video looks good, I guess. Seems to have the requisite ingredients of a pop video: large vacant lot or open space, lip-synching with feeling, dancing around in the middle of said open space, lots of camera angles and saturated color to keep you interested in watching a person dancing around in an open space. But the big thing our new leader notices is, well . . .

"Awesome, he did something with his hair. I love it."

The product manager concurs, "Yeah, isn't it awesome?"

The various foot soldiers and other product managers feel it's safe to start saying what they think, too.

"Oh, wow! I knew something was different. That's so much better."

"Yeah, wow . . ."

"I was about to just point-blank ask him to do something with it." (Laughter)

"That's awesome."

"He looks so much better."

His hair's pretty good, I suppose; a sensible short cut that you could kind of wear either disheveled or combed, depending on the situation. The rest of the video drifts by, and so does the meeting. Before we file out and walk back down the halls to all our respective hiding places, some people ask questions about the sale rumors. Ms. Chocolate Chip states each question before answering; a universal sign that things are not going well. She occasionally has a strange lapse in confidence that makes her take the shades off for a minute, but then she slips them right back on.

"So, have we . . . heard anything?" This from an assistant seated against the back wall.

"Have we heard anything. Well, yes, we've heard a lot."

"Is the sale going through?"

"Is the sale going through. Well, we're just going to have to wait and see right now. There's still some approval process, and even then, we're not sure . . . you know, things could change, things could stay the same, so . . ."

Someone from the art department hands Ms. Chocolate Chip some proofs of photos of Ryan.

"I'll look at these when we're done and get back to you. Thanks, baby."

Baby.

Baby!

With shades on!

Indoors!

It's like backward day; the pop star gets a sensible haircut that makes the marketing team happy, and the executive is wearing shades indoors and calling people "baby." The meeting wraps up and we all do the slow shuffle down the halls and back to offices and cubicles.

———————

There are a few trade magazines in my mailbox, so I grab them and sit down in my office to read them. The story has moved forward. The grandson of the booze mogul is now making it clear in the press that if the sale is approved, he has plans to cut at least a thousand employees in hopes of finding $250 million in cost savings once the deal is officially closed. He has also made clear his plans to cut a lot of bands from contracts, also to help get that $250 million in savings. Everyone knows it's going to be a bloodbath. Nicknames for this guy are already floating around the floor, ranging from the obvious franchised antagonists like Dr. Evil to the basic standbys like Whitey and the Man. It's brought to my attention, by an honorable intern using the Internet to apply due diligence to researching our potential new owner, that he has been something of a lyricist in the past. Love songs — slow jams, it turns out. Holy Christ, it just keeps getting better. Ladies and gentleman, the man who is about to fire me and 999 other employees would like to drop a sexy, heartfelt number on you. He wants to lay it down real nice and slow for you with a ditty about love that he wrote for Celine Dion. It's called "To Love You More," and it goes a little something like this . . .

> Take me back in the arms I love
> Need me like you did before
> Touch me once again

And remember when
There was no one that you wanted more

Don't go you know you will break my heart
He won't love you like I will
I'm the one who'll stay
When he walks away
And you know I'll be standing here still

I'll be waiting for you
Here inside my heart
I'm the one who wants to love you more
You will see I can give you
Everything you need
Let me be the one to love you more

See me as if you never knew
Hold me so you can't let go
Just believe in me
I will make you see
All the things that your heart needs to know

I'll be waiting for you
Here inside my heart
I'm the one who wants to love you more
You will see I can give you
Everything you need
Let me be the one to love you more

And some way all the love that we had can be saved
Whatever it takes we'll find a way
I'll be waiting for you
Here inside my heart

I'm the one who wants to love you more
You will see I can give you
Everything you need
Let me be the one to love you more

There's this part of me that wants to believe everything our new owner is saying to me in his song. I mean, he's clearly a guy with feelings like any other human being on the planet. It's a little awkward, but I feel like I would imagine the woman character in this song feels when she hears these words. In other words, I hope he means what he says. I mean, I want to believe him. I want to, as he puts it, "let him be the one to love me more," as opposed to the guy who's going to put me and everyone else around here out of a job. God, this must be what women feel like when they're dating a songwriter. I wonder if this is how Vallerie felt when she was dating a songwriter. I mean, you just, you want to believe all the things he's saying about love, and his heart, and his ability to be the one to love you more. But the second we buy into it, we're afraid we'll get burned. So we keep our guard up and protect our hearts. Don't we, ladies? Yes. Yes, we do.

NOT A CREATURE STIRRED.
NOT EVEN AN EXECUTIVE DRESSED AS A COP
HANDING OUT SPEEDING TICKETS

So, Vallerie is officially packed up and out of the building now, but while she was here all those years, she had an annual tradition that marked the holidays — a party in her office overlooking Rockefeller Center, on the evening of the Rockefeller Center tree lighting. Now that Ms. Chocolate Chip is the new sheriff in town, she's moved her stuff into Vallerie's corner office, and is keeping the tradition alive. I walk down the hall and right into her lair. Everything is in full swing and the central focus of the soirée is watching a collection of videos from back in the day. We all take to watching one-hit wonders who have faded and bygone hopefuls who never made it.

A sobering education, this reel of videos; feels like it could be part of a "Scared Straight" outreach program to kids thinking about signing record contracts with major labels. They're sort of like fashion knock-offs, these bands in the videos, made up to look like what was supposed to be the next big thing at the time. We've got young cute female rap trios that aren't TLC, sultry divas who were born with only one name but aren't Madonna, a gaggle of toned and chest-hairless boy-men who are not the Backstreet Boys. At the moment there's a video on the screen that must be twenty-five years old. It's an act that might as well have been named Also-a-Cute-Female-Rap-Trio-with-Big-Loud-Colorful-Clothing. I can't recognize them for anything. Jesus, one-hit wonder is one thing, but we are literally watching a no-hit wonder. Maybe even a no-album-was-actually-ever-released-after-we-signed-them wonder.

Everyone in the room is cracking up; we're all having a big laugh, and the more serious and sexy the girls on screen try to be, the harder it is to keep from laughing. They're doing some super-sassy, serious-but-playful, sexy dancing around in an alley where eighties fashion-model types are dressed in torn jeans and kind of brightly colored hooker clothes, leaning against the picture-perfect graffiti-stained brick walls and smoking cigarettes. They look on in a sexy, jaded way as the Unrecognizable American Rap-Trio seem to be trying to get their message across even though the TV is on "mute" and the party is drowning them out. They dance and posture around on the perfectly wet-down asphalt that's reflecting neon lights, they move in and out of the alley cluttered up with new wave hookers, and push their faces up near the camera lens, making it clear they could either make love to you or kill you with their hip-hop prowess.

I try to move in and make a comment to Ms. Chocolate Chip. I lie to myself that my late-in-the-game outgoing gestures of nervous goodwill toward her are some kind of spiritual progress, a sign of enlightenment or something. She stands watching the screen intently, drinking from a small clear plastic cup, holding something small and square on a napkin that she's maybe planning on nibbling on. It looks like, maybe, a little puff pastry? Filled with cheese? Jesus, don't ask her about the snack. The last thing I need is another food-based showdown like when I met her way back on my first day here. I stand next to her, also watching the screen intently. I wait a few beats, sizing up the video with a quiet grin. This is the time. She is thinking the same things I am. Say something.

"Oh, boy. Jeeez. It's kind of strange, isn't it? I mean, standing here, sure it's funny, watching and everything, but at the end of the day our commitment to artists is . . ."

"Shhhh!"

"Oh. Whoops."

"Here it is, you guys!" she hollers out to the room.

Something's about to happen on screen. The anonymous eighties female rappers have bid a sassy farewell to Smoking Big-Haired Cynical Hooker Alley and are now speeding along in a car. Speeding and rapping, driving playfully reckless as images of streets and traffic are projected behind them. I'm not sure what they're running from. One of the hookers could've freaked them out, perhaps. I try to discreetly strike up a conversation again. Quietly this time, just between us.

"You know, I wonder where they're driving to and if the . . ."

"Okay, get ready everyone!" she screams.

"Yeah, okay . . ."

"Keep your eyes on the cop when they get pulled over, everybody!" she hollers again.

Jesus, right in my ear, with the yelling. I think my equilibrium is permanently damaged. I bet if I try to walk away in a straight line, I'll just be walking in tight circles around the snack table.

The car lights up with red and blue lighting. The images projected behind the car start slowing down, then stop. The rapper girls look like everyone looks when they get pulled over, but sexier. Kind of like, "We're getting pulled over, but we're just gonna go ahead and let this police officer know that we're an intoxicating combination of playful, angry, and sexy."

When the cop walks up to the car, everyone at the party screams. It's this big-shot executive from upstairs. The guy who signed Twisted Sister and Kid Rock and matchbox twenty. (Note to editor: please leave that last band name all lowercase, otherwise their manager calls up screaming about how their name is to appear all lowercase. And I mean SCREAMING. Trust me on this.) Somebody unmutes the TV just in time to hear him deliver his line about how the rapper girls were speeding and how he'll need to see their licenses. Then everyone starts laughing so loudly that I can't hear how the sexy anonymous rappers get fresh with him, but it looks like they got off the hook. The video ends, the party chatter resumes, and me and Ms. Chocolate Chip are finally able to have a moment to chat and catch up with each other a bit.

"Ah, that was funny. Classic, right? Hey, great party, by the way. Good move. Hope you do it again next year."

"I will, if any of us are even still working here."

———————

Okay, then.

Auto Flash and the Darkness

First of all, I don't understand this band called the Darkness. I've watched the band's video about a thousand times in the process of going about making a television commercial for them, and I'm still confused. The lead singer is a guy in a fluorescent pink dancewear unitard thing that is cut low and hints at showing you the flames tattooed above his penis. The bassist looks sort of like every janitor of every public school I ever attended, save for the fact that his shtick in the video we're watching seems to be walking like a robot and wearing a Kamikaze headband. And in the video, while the singer wrestles on the floor near a ring of flames with a woman who looks like Satan — far away from the big tentacles of the space alien thing that's trying to kill them all — the lead guitarist (no leotard, headband, or shtick — *that* must've been a tense band meeting) simply plays long solos and casually takes note of the ensuing battle. Your first thought, if you're anything like me, is that this is some kind of post–Spinal Tap brilliant rock-and-roll irony. Your initial reaction is kind of like, "Ha! That's awesome!" with this sort of half grin on your face, as if you're in on the joke. Right, but then you hear how pissed off they get when anyone in the office assumes that this stuff they're doing is some kind of funny joke, and then what are you supposed to think about them?

There's the story floating around here about when the band

showed up at the offices once and someone in the A&R department basically made a comment something to the extent of, "You're totally in character, even in a meeting. I love it!" The confused and upset reaction from the band and their management prompted much company-wide discussion about how the man in the hot pink spandex jumpsuit barely concealing his fiery crotch, and his friend the robotic janitor man, are *not* being ironic. They are being serious, they have sold loads of records in the U.K., and they should be treated accordingly.

They're coming around here again, promoting the record, plus they've got a hit single in the States right now. They'll be doing an in-store performance in Times Square at the Virgin Megastore. And the usual e-mail gets sent out to everyone in the company, saying you should show up and support the in-store performance. I usually dodge these e-mails when they come around, especially when they ask us to stand out in front of MTV holding signs up in the air as if we're fans waiting outside for whatever Time Warner recording artist is showing up that day to promote something. I read those e-mails and wonder how this is really fooling anyone. I mean, do people walking around in Times Square see the likes of us standing there with the perfectly preprinted "homemade" signs and think, "Oh, I guess the young pop artist that's coming to MTV's studio today is not only a hit with the fifteen- to eighteen-year-olds, but it seems they have quite a contingency of die-hard fans who are thirty-one- to fifty-year-old office workers." Anyway, a lot of people from the office are going to the Darkness in-store performance, and I figure I probably should, too. Especially with all the talk of a merger and people getting laid off. It's probably a really good time to start becoming a gung-ho employee. In my head I'm imagining best-case scenarios like this:

New Owner: "I think we can fire most of the marketing department, don't you, Investment Partner?"

Investment Partner: "Not so fast. Did you see how enthusiastic and supportive Employee Number 2991 was at the Darkness in-store performance? He was even taking pictures."

See, I've recently bought this camera. A great camera, I think. Not some huge pro camera or anything, but a pretty nice, okay, yes, totally automatic point-and-shoot camera. And the idea in my head, unfortunately, is that I will show up at the event, get some kind of press credentials from one of the people I work with, and take great pictures of this band that will in turn make investors and analysts realize I'm quite an asset to the company and should be kept on after the sale and takeover. So, off I go, carrying one of these little I LOVE NEW YORK plastic bags that stores use around here; it's got my film in it, and in my other hand I'm carrying my little point-and-shoot camera.

I walk into the Virgin Megastore in Times Square and get to the stairs, where I immediately bump into Jackie, a very kind, hard-working foot soldier from the video production department who has propped up many a glorified middle manager's success; perfect.

I try to indicate that I'll need some extra access to this event by holding my plastic shopping bag up a little bit.

"What's this? Do you need me to hold this or . . . ?"

"No, it's my film."

"Are you shooting band stills?"

"Well, no, not officially. Yes. I am, yeah."

Jackie gets on her walkie-talkie.

"I need one laminate — photo access — to the front of the main stairs, please. Copy?"

The walkie-talkie crackles to life with a reply. "Copy that, we're coming to you with one laminate for photographer."

My eyes dart over to the photo pit. Holy Christ, those guys in there are *serious*. There must be a hundred of them, all jockeying aggressively for position, all with super long lenses and vests with a million pockets loaded with film and whatever other accessories you can get for a camera like theirs. For mine all you can get is a better case made out of soft leather — it's a little better than the case it comes with, so I sprung for it — and you can also get this mini tripod that fits on the bottom, neither of which have required me to get a vest like the ones all of these guys have. They have light meters hanging around their necks. Good one, never thought of that.

"You know what, actually, Jackie? I might only be doing photo, uh, shooting for, like, a second."

Into her walkie-talkie: "Correction. I need one photo access plus one VIP all-access. Thank you."

To me: "That way you can go wherever you want. Not just the pit."

The passes arrive, and for a minute I daydream about how many other concerts I wish I had these passes for. But tickets are a joke at work. The only people who seem get tickets to shows are the mega-senior bigshots from way upstairs. Anyone else, forget it. Although, one time I bought a huge bottle of expensive booze for an intern and he got me a set of tickets to a surprise club show by Foo Fighters from somebody across town at RCA.

Passes go around neck, and I go around to the photographer pit.

"Hi, guys."

There is, it turns out, a look that an entire pit of grizzled New York newspaper photographers can all affect at the same time in order to convey that they're not above using physical force with the likes of you.

I barely take my camera out of the optional soft leather case and dig into my plastic shopping bag for a roll of film and they give me the aforementioned look.

Okay, I get it. God.

I don't even bother getting past the periphery of them. I put my "equipment" into my coat pocket and head out of there, off and up to the left. Past a blocked-off aisle of comedy DVDs on sale, past some books about reality TV shows, through a display of T-shirts, hats, and condoms (*Goddamn, I thought they said this place was a record store*) and around a stack of cases for the band's guitars, and . . . okay, wait . . . I'm on stage. The side of it, actually, next to two big racks containing about two dozen of the band's guitars. Jesus, how many guitars do you need to play "Get Your Hand Off My Woman" and "I Believe in a Thing Called Love"?

I look up from the guitars and right across from me, on the other side of the stage, in a glass room that looks to be some kind of manager's office turned into a VIP suite, is every one of my bosses looking across the stage. Seems I've positioned myself right in their line of sight, directly on the other side of the stage. Look: there's Dick, and Ms. Chocolate Chip, a gaggle of copresidents and cochairmen, the band's management; everyone who's anyone, really. We're locked in a kind of long-distance direct stare, as if the distance across the stage is just enough to make each of us wonder if we're looking at each other. *Quick. Think. Why are you up here? Justify it.* I slowly take my camera out of my pocket, remove it from its soft leather carrying case, and do some autofocusing. I fire off a few shots with auto flash and the anti–red eye feature, even though there's nobody on stage yet.

Suddenly the band is on stage. All I can hear myself think-ing — in a voice strangely like my mother's for some reason — is, *Oh, my. Whoops.* You never realize it, but being so close to the running around, the posing mid-guitar solo, and the loud yelling for the audience to "put your hands together" — it's all a little too close for comfort. Like being cramped right up against the weird guy on the subway singing for spare change.

I'm on the far left side of the stage, sort of leaning/sitting against a waist-high case of cables, right next to the rack of guitars that their roadie guy will reach into between songs, pick one from, then tune it and run it out to the guitarist on-stage. The lead singer looks over to the guitarist to make a rockin' face in appreciation of his big blistering rock-and-roll solo. He turns, he makes his eyes kind of squinted and puckers up his lips as if he's saying, "Ooooh!" I'm, you know, looking in that direction. He seems to look past the guitarist, and for a split second his puckered-up, squinting rock-and-roll face turns into a bit of a "who's that guy on the side of the stage over there" face. I smile politely. In hopes of explaining things a bit, I pull my little camera up to my eye and take a couple of shots of him.

The guys in the photo pit are giving me that evil look of theirs. With all of the ruckus, I can't tell if the bosses are all still staring straight at me; I looked once right when the guys in the band started making the audience put their hands up over their heads and clap to the beat again. As far as I could tell when I looked, everyone on the other side of the stage behind the glass was sipping little clear plastic cups of wine or little green bottles of mineral water, eating cheese and grapes from the catering trays. A roadie runs by me with a guitar that he hands to the lead singer, just in time for him to start playing his own blistering rock-and-roll guitar solo. Then another roadie appears right down in front of the stage and gives the lead singer playing the guitar solo a tired look of, "Okay, ready? Let's do our little thing we do." I'm still leaning up against the case of cables on the left of the stage, and the lead singer walks up to the front edge of the stage and lets his legs fall, one after the other, over the roadie's shoulders, chicken-fight style. The roadie then walks through the crowd with the singer on his shoulders, and, thankfully, the rest of the crowd now look as awkward as me about being too close to the action. I take a second to enjoy having a little breathing room up here with the attention off the stage. After a pass through the crowd, the roadie backs up against the stage like a tired, patient father carrying a kid who's starting to get too big for this game. The lead singer hops off of him and runs to the mic like a kid getting off a bike and running inside for dinner.

The band finishes the song with a huge, extremely loud, picture-perfect stadium-rock grand finale. As guitars are still fading, and ears are still ringing, they all meet at the front edge of the stage, join hands and raise their arms in triumph, then they all thrust downward into a bow at exactly the same time, repeat it once, then walk off stage waving a casual wave, well aware of the hurricane that they created. I make my way out of the store and into the middle of Times Square. I stand there in the stuttering glow of the city's schizophrenic fit of neon billboards, right in the center of one of the greatest cities in the world, where anything is possible and so many people's hopes and dreams have come true. I am hoping and dreaming that my bosses thought I was enthusiastic and supportive.

We Won't Get Fooled Again.
I'm Kidding. Obviously,
We'll Get Fooled Again

Here's a good riddle:

Q: Without using your watch or any personal consumer electronics, how can you tell how much time has passed while you sit in the same meetings time after time, never sure of what they accomplish, in an office building that you come to every day even though you feel it's impossible to affect change in a large corporate setting, precisely because succeeding in a corporate environment is based largely on blending in?

A: Look in the bathroom mirror at home this weekend and notice that you are visibly a year older, yet again.

I know you're probably saying, "That's not such a good riddle, Mr. Bad Attitude." Or maybe, "That's a terrible riddle, Mr. Better-Get-with-the-Program." But it's the kind of riddle that springs to mind after walking past a huge sign that says TIME & LIFE every morning, thinking about how both of them are flying by, then riding an elevator up in order to sit at a desk or conference table all day again.

Welcome to a very special edition of the sales and marketing meeting. Everyone has taken seats, the entire company this time, top to bottom. We fall into a caste system something like inmates in a prison mess hall; if you're big, you take a seat near the head of the table anchored in next to a co-something. If you're just sort of big, you take a seat at the table a few down from that. If you're middling or anywhere else on the food chain, you sit in the folding temporary chairs along the wall.

Everyone is talking, Palm Piloting, etc. Then the last few big guys file in. Hey, no way — check it out. Look! It's that guy! I've seen him on the cover of all the trade magazines that have been covering the sale and merger! They keep saying he's the guy the new owner will make chairman of the entire Warner Music Group. I guess it's official then; this guy's the new chairman. Which must mean that the deal went through and our new owner has officially bought us. Everything's changing so fast.

He's tall. Maybe six foot four, handsome, graying cropped hair, a solid tan. He *looks* like the next chairman of a music company, the same way they said Harding looked like the next president of the United States. Do you ever wonder how much more would come your way if you were a little bit taller with slightly more symmetrical facial features? I mean, not so good-looking that it would throw you into a crazy sexed-up tailspin of quadrupled income and bad decisions, but just a little more attractive. Just, say, 20 percent more attractive — enough to get maybe an extra 20 percent of the good things in life and career. An extra three days of paid vacation, maybe; a 20 percent tip added on to each paycheck, one in twenty people going out of their way to flirt with you; a 20 percent edge on getting the promotion. Have you ever really just sat and thought about how it would change things? Well, my advice to you is, don't sit there thinking about it while you're staring right at the new chairmen of the entire company, because it looks like you're enamored with him, or challenging him, or something.

The meeting settles and he introduces himself. He has an accent. Of course. Jesus, what else, an assistant named Ursula and an Austin Healy with a telephone in the glove box? We get it; you're a winner.

After introducing himself with an effortless charm and getting a few eager laughs, he leans back in his chair, casually crosses one leg over the other, and says, "I have a question for everybody here. Is this band, the Darkness, a novelty band? Or, let me put it this way: Are they in danger of being *perceived* as a novelty band?"

What I wish I would've said:

"Well, sir, the lead singer alternates his wardrobe between bright pink leather pants and a spandex unitard. I've got a snapshot of him riding through a crowd on a roadie's shoulders, shirtless and sticking out his tongue like a cross between Nigel Tuffnel from Spinal Tap and an oversexed Benny Hill sketch. And the video we watched in this room not so long ago is all about his trying to escape a big octopus in outer space as a female Satan tempts him into a fiery ring, and the bassist walks around like a robot with a penchant for ninja headbands. If that answers your question."

That would've been a sweet moment. But I'm afraid it went down a little more like this:

He asks his question, "I have a question for everybody here. Is this band, the Darkness, a novelty band? Or, let me put it this way: Are they in danger of being *perceived* as a novelty band?"

I look sort of toward him. I continue looking in his general direction with a polite smile and a "Hmmm, good question" look on my face, not saying anything, but kind of looking up at the ceiling like I'm really pondering it. Like a very smart employee would. The kind of employee who should never be laid off. While I do this, other people answer.

"Well, actually, that's what some of us here thought at first, but they're really into what they do, and we're really excited to be working on this record," says a woman in the middle ground of the radio or video promotions department.

A guy from the sales department, I think: "I can certainly see what you're saying. It's a good question. I think ultimately, people are reacting to the music well in research, and we're definitely seeing good numbers so far. It is a good question, though. At the end of the day, we're working this record well, and we're seeing it start to happen, but it is a good question. "

Try to speak. Stop looking at the ceiling and tell him he's asked a good question! He's the new chairman!

From a person in the publicity department: "I think there's an education process with this band."

I continue tilting my head, looking upward in different directions to hopefully look like I'm thinking about the question.

President Harding speaks up again.

"Okay. I just wanted to hear your opinions. I'm just kind of getting my feet on the ground . . . getting a read on things."

I finally speak up.

"Ah, okay," I mouth silently.

My mouth then returns to being closed into a mild and polite smile. I sit there hoping to God this whole thing was some kind of secret litmus test that I passed. I try to tell myself that it was a trick question, and the trick is that, in fact, there was no right answer . . . and that only smart, valuable employees would know that, and that's why the new chairman asked it. I try to act like the trick question was actually devised to see who would be dumb enough to try to answer it, and that's who he and the new billionaire owner will fire, because what they're really looking for are quiet, thoughtful people who stare at the ceiling thinking about things. I try to tell myself a lot of things these days that I'm not buying.

He goes on to tell us a bunch of stuff about how record companies are no longer in the music business, but the *lifestyle* business.

He says something like, "I don't tell people I'm in the record business. I tell people I'm in the business of delivering a *lifestyle*; hooded sweatshirts and other merchandise — merch that features various band logos; licensing; soft drinks; everything. There is no limit to how this business will change and become a business of selling a way of living, more than simply selling music."

Filing out of the conference room once again, I think I'll do something else instead of going back to my office and reading news stories about our now certain mass layoffs. I head down to the lobby to go outside and take a walk around the block to clear my head. To clear my way of living . . . my *lifestyle*.

Downstairs, I'm walking through the lobby, heading for the giant revolving doors of this building — that's when I see a little piece of history that maybe nobody else will ever see: Rush Hair is walking out of the building slowly, a little lost in thought maybe, and . . . wait, this is the walk of a man who is walking out of the building for the very last time, isn't it? Somehow, there's no mistaking it. I stop and watch from the front doors as he walks away down a long white corridor and off to some exit that I never use that probably goes to underground executive parking for the big names upstairs. He gets smaller and smaller on the horizon as he walks away with a slow, you-don't-need-to-call-security gait. The rest of the building's lobby is buzzing with people doing other things; people that work in other offices, on other floors, in other businesses that are still alive and kicking. It's a rather random Thursday afternoon, without ceremony or even re- markable weather outside. Basically a completely average and unremarkable looking day — but that's almost always the kind of day it is in life when an era ends, isn't it?

Uncool Merch Ideas for Bands

Chef's classic bib apron with adjustable neckband, band pictured on front.

Logo sport coat.

Leather day planner with gold embossed band logo on front.

Executive weather desk clock with hygrometer, thermometer, and barometer — attractive pewter band logo on cherry wood base.

Old-fashioned gumball machine with eleven-inch glass top displaying band logo and silhouette of each member.

Sixteen-ounce spill-proof "commuter"-style aluminum beverage cup. Band logo on lid and tour dates on front and sides.

Logo bath towel set.

Wooden backscratcher featuring current album artwork.

Attractive photo frame desk clock that displays picture of band.

SMASH HIT

The phone in my office is ringing. I answer and it's one of the *two* assistants who sit outside the remaining label president's office. Remaining, because there was another one of him only weeks ago. A copresident. But that copresident was fired, cut, canned, and sacked. I have to say, I love all the sort of hard-boiled detective words for "laid off" that we've been able to use in these last days in the middle-aged and paunchy belly of this stumbling, disconnected, dying beast. I want to embrace the language even more. I want to break the modern corporate silence and fear in the halls here by talking out of the side of my mouth and wearing a sturdy fedora. I want to walk right up to the slickest, most well-groomed, over-educated, Rolex-wearing, Prada-clad, modern-day record executive in the building and bark a nineteen-forties film noir pulp bravado. "Did you hear about Frank? Canned. Yes sir, canned, caboodled, and strong-armed right out of this high-rise hothouse and straight home to his Sally Jane for repair. Why, he'll spend a day in the gin mill and be good as new."

In these sterile, feeble, insecure, and uncertain corridors I want to remember a time when people were fired and the first thing they thought about was a stiff upper lip and a good poker face for the wife and kids. Jesus, if my dad would've ever come home and announced he'd been fired, something tells me that my sister and I would've been *excited* about what the future might hold; about what he might come up with next and how it would be better than the last job he had. He is that kind of man, from that time. But in this so-called rock-and-roll company that I have found myself working in for the last year and a half, all we have managed to muster is to sit in offices awaiting a phone call that we all knew was coming for the last six months based on what we've read almost daily in the *Wall Street Journal* and various music trade magazines. We sit, fattened on expense accounts, and try to figure out what our severance packages will add up to be. What our prorated annual bonuses will be. What our "difficult transition" bonuses will be. And no matter how big of a number it all adds up to, it will look thin next to our new boss's *$50 million* five-year salary that he recently . . . *WHAT!* I've been feeling guilty for not using both sides of the paper in the printer! We've been asked not to expense work meals for the month because there's no money! Jesus, $50 million sounds like a joke amount. Like you're complaining about your new boss getting "a gajillion, zillion dollars" or something. Fifty-million-dollar contract for the new boss, Ms. Chocolate Chip wearing sunglasses in the marketing meeting—have the executives become the rock stars? And what am I not understanding in my little Homer Simpson brain about the difficult financial times reportedly plaguing the record business? Maybe my definition of hard times isn't the same as the record business's definition of hard times. For me, hard times were punctuated with phrases like "If I return those bottles for the deposit, I can buy some cheese."

"He wants to see you in his office," this from the voice on the other end of the phone.

The one thing that always makes me happy about taking the elevator here is that they have these little flat-screen TV things inside and you can watch national weather highlights, read a quote from somebody famous, or get a health and fitness tip. And somehow, over the last year and half, these little flat-screens have put things in perspective on weird days. Like, if you have a meeting that feels like it could be the meeting you are going to get fired in, you can look on this little flat-screen and see that a snowstorm in Denver has killed three people and that eating one piece of fruit a day will reduce your chances of heart disease. And you feel the surge of confidence and gratitude that comes from knowing you're not dead in a blizzard in Denver and that you have a chance at beating cardiac arrest by hucking a big hard apple at the Grim Reaper and nailing him right on the side of his head.

So, I'm watching the screen and there is a small delusion of reprieve as I start my descent. The same small voice in my head that told me maybe working for a major record label in New York would be the most exciting rock-and-roll thing I had ever encountered in my life-long love affair with music is trying to convince me this wasn't my first and *last* trip to the remaining copresident's office. It said, "Hey, this could be one of those classic rock-and-roll moments that you've been dreaming of since you were nine! This could be the kind of thing where you walk into an office of aged luminaries sipping scotch and inviting you into a conversation about the time Led Zeppelin did something crazy that nobody knows about because it was covered up and hidden from the press at great expense. It could be the type of thing where it takes you a second to realize the guy on the couch in the corner is Mick Jagger or Jimmy Page or, you know . . . at least *somebody* other than another well-heeled seven-figure-hording heavy hitter." Me and the tiny voice would even maybe settle for Jewel's mom/manager

or even the drummer from Hootie and the Blowfish at this
point. Anybody, if it meant that this ominous meeting could
at least be a little bit like the kind of rock-and-roll moment
that seems so sadly missing in this newly merged, trimmed,
refinanced, restructured, freshly scrubbed, wide-eyed, suited
and tied record company.

I step out of the elevator, and past his floor's magnetized,
frosted-glass double doors with a swipe of my ID card. I walk
by the two assistants and into his office. I recall that in a rush
of recent developments, this remaining copresident has been
renamed new cochairman. Jesus, if the new head of the entire
company is getting $50 million, I'll bet you Co-Whatever-His-
Title-Is still nails, at the very minimum, a couple million a year
in these tough times. When I enter his office, Co-Man is seated
behind his desk in the quiet, high-above-the-streets-now hum
of expensive art, recessed lighting, and . . . God, this . . . *desk*.

Racing through my head:

- *Jesus,* look at it. Stare at it like an eclipse they told you not
  to look directly at, because this is your only chance.
- I didn't know they made desks like this. It's, like, *Huge*.
  And round. Lacquered, shiny wood and metal. Like a
  cross between a private-jet interior, a Four Seasons presi-
  dential suite, a yacht, and a luxury tour bus.
- Okay, turn away. Stop staring at it.
- Good God, man, stop it! He can see you staring right at it.
  He's sitting on the other side of it. If you looked up right
  now you'd see him watching you.
- Just act like you thought there was a crack in it. Act like
  you've seen desks like this all the time.
- Look at it, though. Seriously. Look at this thing!

And there's a woman seated next to him. Think. Who is she, dammit? Do you recognize her? Maybe she's a singer of some sort. Although she is very sensible in her little pantsuit, lacquered and tamed Aqua Net hairdo, and very sober shoes. Maybe that's the next big thing, though. Maybe Sensible Divas are it, and the Co-Man knows this and he's going to be like, "Dan, meet our newest star . . . *Carol*. One name. Like 'Jewel' or 'Madonna' but more sensible. And your job, as Director of Creative Development, is to help introduce her to the world. We'll need Carol ad campaigns. We'll need a Carol video. What should Carol's look be? Should she *always* be in the Carol pantsuit and leather loafers, or does she mix it up with navy pleated skirts and blouses? I don't know. I'm not the creative guy . . . *that's your job*."

She looks at me. And I look at the desk some more. I swear to you this desk had to cost north of fifty grand. And another thought crosses my mind in a rushed daydream, in which, with perfect pitch and without a waver in my voice, I say, "We have to sell your desk, sir. We're firing assistants that make less than we could get for this thing used." But I snap back to reality when Carol announces my name and title.

"Dan Kennedy, Director of Creative Development." She says it like some Human Resources woman.

Oh, right. Human. Resources. Uh-oh.

And then Mr. Co-Hyphen-Question-Mark starts a thing about me. A little ditty that he kind of makes up on the spot like a toastmaster covering for a drunk toastmaster friend who ditched out of his home-meeting speaking obligation at the last minute. "Dan, your work at Atlantic Records has been . . . extraordinary." (Seriously? I didn't even think this guy knew I worked here. He always ignored me in the elevator and stuff.) "And you've certainly done some incredible" — looks down at list in front of him — "cre . . . ative . . . creative developing . . . development directing . . . anyway, I think you know what I'm trying to say: You're very talented."

And Carol echoes him, seeing his "very talented" and raising him one "extremely talented" as she nods her head and focuses her eyes on middle distance like they do in inspirational scenes in the movies. Co-Man resumes.

"Your work here has been more than we could've hoped for." (So *this* is what it must feel like to win an award or something. I swear, at this moment, I think that maybe with all of the restructuring that's happening, I'm actually getting promoted.) "You've brought so much energy to your job here — andtodaywillbeyourlastday — and because you've gone really rather above and beyond in your duties here, I would like you to know that I plan on still contracting you on a freelance level more or less, perhaps in the future, if the opportunity should arise, possibly, if it should work out, to some degree."

Whoa! Did we all hear that? Did Carol hear it? I heard it. Crammed in there between the flattering stuff and the strange, politically safe, benign, and very vague promise to use me on a future project, he . . . he . . . totally canned me. Carol swings into action fast and deft, like the tranquilizer dart will wear thin soon and she has to work quickly while I still have a pleasant and dazed look. She points to documents bearing my signature and figures and dates. She smiles when she tells me how long I will remain on payroll until my official termination starts and then how long I will be paid in severance and how long my health insurance will continue to last. I

make some strained joke about wanting to undergo a cosmetic
surgery that most doctors are "currently describing as an elec-
tive vanity surgery" and they just kind of give me a gentle and
supportive look and explain to me that it would most likely be
covered. This makes my mind race to try and figure out what
about me is so obviously askew that a plastic surgery joke falls
flat.

   In the middle of all of this, I feel my stomach fall and my
blood go a bit thin, because no matter what anybody says, and
no matter how much you expect it, and no matter how you
tell yourself you can take it, when you are fired, you feel it.
The two words everyone here throws around with no apparent relation to high demand now ricochet around my head
and in the hollow feeling in my chest: Smash! Hit! And as
he sits behind his desk waiting for Carol to finish her part of
the show, Co-Co — if I may start to refer to him on more casual terms — glances down at the sheet in front of him, looks
mildly confused, and adds one last and late sentence to his
praise of me and my extraordinary talent:

   "And, Dan, um . . . refresh me on what it is you did in your
role here."

   Jesus. What?

   So I tell him that I have a background in New York advertising, and first worked here as a freelancer. I tell him that
what I do here is . . . *Did. Was.* What I *did* here *was* write
and produce television advertising campaigns for our artists,
wrote print advertising and marketing materials, came up
with partnership ideas here and there. There was the idea I
had for developing artists with an online contract — I remind
him that we were on a big video conference call together about
that idea, because he said he was really excited about the idea

and wanted me to explain it to the people in the L.A. office. I tell him that I had put together some partnership deals, one with JVC in North America that resided in at least the "pretty lucrative" file. Certainly justified my year's salary, anyway. And I'm telling him all about this stuff and somehow actually, strangely, starting to feel my self-esteem come back up a little, even though I'm canned now. And this is augmented by seeing a look sweep across his face that seems to say, "Ah, right, right. Okay . . ." as if he suddenly remembers. And that maybe I wasn't supposed to be on the list? Or maybe the look on his face isn't about me at all and he's just remembering what he wants to have for lunch, like, "Yes, sushi. Ooooh, and there's that new Japanese place downstairs that just opened last week." I look at how many papers the legal department has drawn up and how many places my signature is needed, and then it hits me again, a little aftershock about how final all this is.

When we're done, I step out of his office and the huge door begins closing behind me. It's a large, heavy, solid door that feels like the gate to a Wall Street titan's lair. It reeks of stale, dubious deals done years ago that have finally stopped paying unreal dividends, blind and half-empty star-making promises, and of this label's biggest, most relevant rock-and-roll glory days, which are now almost thirty years behind it. His two assistants sit at smallish desks that match the color and grain of the door closing behind me, looking at computer screens and trying not to make eye contact. The door notches into its deep and locked grooves and makes a sound too permanent and solid to be called a click, and when it does, they finally look up at me. I am stunned, and I'm still holding my gray envelope with my name on it. And we all know what the gray envelope is. And I steady my voice and chest to say something to the assistants.

"Well, that was very awkward. But, there's a lot of change going on. And starting tomorrow morning . . . you both work for *me*."

They look at me wide-eyed in shock; and albeit a little too late, this job finally feels a little bit like rock and roll.

How to Plan a Bloodbath

By the time I get back to my office to start packing it, I realize that everyone's phones have been ringing like mine did. The floor is abuzz with chaos, assistants carrying huge rolls of bubble wrap, tape guns, stacks of boxes waiting to be assembled and filled. Ms. Chocolate Chip yells something, very emotionally, almost prime-time-network-drama in tone, to nobody in particular about how, "They're going to do this to you, too! To everybody!" and slams her door. Closet doors that I've never seen opened are being unlocked, and swung open — and behind each door is everything that just over a thousand people will need to move their offices into their apartments in short order. Stacks of boxes, cases of shipping tape and tape guns, fifty-yard rolls of bubble wrap stacked end to end, rolls of shipping labels from the company paid to courier our belongings home, all locked away in the last few weeks or days, probably late at night long after everyone had gone home after six or seven, hidden and waiting for this moment when the trigger is pulled. Weird to think that it was all hiding right next to your office all this time.

Dick walks down the hall and gives me and three foot soldiers from the video production department a strange and impromptu tear-filled farewell. The three of us wonder almost aloud why we're being treated to the epic good-bye, since he probably spoke a total of five or six terse words to any of us during our respective entire stints at the company. I stand there looking somber and respectful, wondering if this means that the rumored huge apartment the label had him set up in on the top of that tower near Columbus Circle has to be packed up, too. Suddenly he needs to assure us about his fate.

"I will be back. This is a big business, and I'll be back," he says through a forced smile and watery eyes.

Thanks for the warning.

"It's a big business. . . . you haven't heard the last of me. I will be back."

Okay. We get it, sport. You'll be back.

Months later, in the unshaven, aimless, unemployed days of summer I'm walking around uptown on Park Avenue, killing time, when I see him. A strangely level playing field on that sidewalk: just two unshaven men doing anything to get out of the house. If I had had the guts, I would've said hello. Instead we avert our eyes and walk on by, the two of us passing each other on an otherwise empty sidewalk in midday, not saying a thing. Exactly the way we used to pass each other in the halls at the office when we had jobs. It feels oddly comforting to know there's one thing that hasn't changed.

My Corporate Good-bye
E-mail Never Sent

Sorry for the mass e-mail, everyone, but, well, after eighteen long, um, months, it's time to move on. If you want to know what the HR woman looks like, drop by my office while I'm packing. You should know who to look for, because if you get called into a meeting and she's the only other one sitting there besides you and a copresident, you're screwed. Trust me.

I will miss you guys! Even the extremely wealthy four or five of you who ignored most of us in the elevators! ;-) Whoa, somebody hasn't had their coffee yet!

Anyway, as we all know, these are challenging times. Not for the mail-order homemade salsa and sauces business (Bob from radio promotions, I think you were right to choose this time to take the leap of faith), but these are certainly challenging times for the record business. Which is why I've made the decision to be moving on (just fired) to bigger and better things. I've always said (usually after drinking a bit more than I'm accustomed to) that part of the fun and adventure in life is not knowing what's around the corner. Well, I'm having a pretty fun and adventurous time, if you get my drift. Did you know that in China, they use the same symbol for both *Crisis* and *Opportunity*? It's really only in our Western culture that we associate being laid off with "bad news" or a "strain on my relationship" or a "lapse in personal hygiene after eighteen

months spent writing at home." If you ask me, I agree with the
Chinese folks, I see the so-called crisis as an opportunity as
well, which is why I'm keeping it pretty upbeat in my good-
bye e-mail.

To that end, like Bob from radio promotions, I've also decided to finally start a small home-based business. Please help
me by filling out this brief survey! Click Reply, and then type
in your answers below before sending! Just evaluate the following statements as either "True," "Somewhat True," or "You
seem like you might be developmentally disabled, but best of
luck with things!" in the blank space under each statement.

1. I would like to buy handmade decorations for my home
   on the Internet, but at the present time, there aren't many
   options for me online.

2. While I enjoy Bob's Tasty Homemade Salsa and Sauces,
   and I like to support former coworkers' new ventures, I
   would be more likely to buy tasteful handmade decorations for my home online than I would a perishable food
   product.

3. I know Susan from video promo was also fired today. I
   would feel better coming to terms with this and other
   distressing job-related information if my work environment featured tasteful handmade decorations.

4. I have an extra room in my home that I would like to
   make available for an Internet-based business that sells
   handmade home and office decorations.

5. I would prefer the barter system as a means of payment
   for renting the extra room, as opposed to cash, especially
   since the items that would be bartered are tasteful, handmade, and of PROFESSIONAL quality.

Thanks for the one and a half years we have worked together, you guys. It was an exciting time, and there are exciting times ahead.

This is exciting!

— Dan in marketing

Office Supplies for the Unemployed

1" Post-it Flags

Available in eleven different colors, the Post-it flag is perfect for marking pages in important presentations, notes, and manuals.

You, the unemployed, of course, have no business whatsoever marking pages in a presentation these days. As a matter of fact, the word *presentation* only applies to you in the context of letting your personal presentation go straight downhill. By the way, waking up at one in the afternoon and pulling on whatever T-shirt you find laying closest to the bed that particular afternoon, then putting on a hat and calling yourself "dressed for the day" is breaking everyone's heart. Trust us. They just don't know how to tell you without hurting your feelings and making the situation worse than it already is.

Easily removed and repositioned, available in economic 100-pack.

Glo-Write Bullet-Tip Dry-Erase Markers

Specially made for dark/black dry-erase boards, available in eye-catching fluorescent white, green, pink, blue, green.

What's that you say? You've never seen a black dry-erase board in a big fancy high-rise conference room where your assistant brings you bottled water and phone messages while you sit in an expensive German chair and try to look smart? Yeah, well, these bad boys are pretty much used to advertise lunch specials and happy-hour cocktails at restaurants — the waiters write the specials on the black dry-erase board, then put it out on the sidewalk. Not so much at the nice places, obviously, but more like the tourist joints; those scrappy little beer-and-clams joints that are always hiring waiters and bartenders. Any of this sinking in, Einstein?

Available in 12- and 24-pack. Ink wipes away with damp cloth — just disappears without a trace. Like everything seems to, sooner or later.

Palm Tungsten™ T Stylus 3-Pack

The new 3-pack means you'll never find yourself without a stylus again.

Ironic, since you've certainly found yourself without a Palm Pilot to use them with. Keep a spare stylus at the office. Ouch. Sorry, you know what we mean, though — just saying you can have them in several places. Keep one in your car or at your house in the country. Ouch. Now we're just screwing with you — seriously, though, what the hell are you doing with your time since the layoffs?

Platinum-Success Leather Day Planner

Keep all of your important dates, meetings, and appointments in one convenient place. Ahhh, Ha Ha Ha, Ha Ha Ha Ha, Ha Ha Ha, Ha Ha Ha Ha Ha Ha Ha Ha, Oh . . . ah . . . haha. Now we're just being plain cruel.

Genuine leather. Month, year, and three-year view. 8 1/2" x 11". For people with jobs.

The Trick Is to Keep Breathing: Trying Meditation Instead of TV Watching

First of all, don't be nervous. And don't stress out. I mean, Jesus, that's the first thing, goddammit! Do. Not. Stress. Out! Okay, breathing break, breathing break. You're already freaking out so let's take a little breathing break.

Take a deep breath.

Do it!

Okay, now count up to ten.

Or is it backward to ten? I think that might be it. Up to ten doesn't sound right. Because you can just race right through it, but backward you would . . . alright, you know what? Screw it. It's already been like fifteen seconds so let's get back to it, quitter.

Okay, so the first thing you want to do is go to your secret place or whatever. Okay . . . secret place. Fuck, apparently my secret place is right here in New York, a collage of the terrorist attacks, weird trash I've seen on the streets over the last ten years, images from that time I saw pigeons pecking at frozen vomit at seven in the morning in the West Village. Damn it! I can't meditate right. But they were eating it. Frozen. Vomit. Jesus. Okay, I'll just go with it. I think it's supposed to be a meadow with a stream, but fine, whatever.

No, forget this. I suck at this. This is not a good secret place. It's seriously supposed to be a meadow or field with horses or something. Okay, the couch; that's my new secret place; I love sitting on the couch and checking my e-mail with my laptop and watching TV.

Bingo. Okay. It's not exactly a stream in a meadow, but at least it's not a terrorist attack or those pigeons. Couch, present-day, it is! Not super secret, this secret place, but visualizing being there is already making me feel better about things. Okay, so . . . picturing the couch . . . pictur . . . ing . . . it . . . okay, good.

We just let our thoughts drift by like they're in a stream. Happy thoughts, maybe. Or even not-so-happy thoughts. I guess that's the thing, if you're meditating right you can let any kind of thought drift by in the stream and be fine with it. Because you are lovingly detached and not needing to change what you think. Any thought can drift past: "Job is gone . . . severance money will be gone soon enough at this rate." Ah, and here comes another lily pad floating by with another thought on it: "What about health insurance?" Just thoughts. True thoughts, granted. Frightening thoughts, sure. But we just notice the thoughts on the lily pads. We don't huck a big god-damn rock at the lily pads, or set them on fire and try to float them back upstream where the stupid thoughts came from, because apparently that's not good meditation. We just simply notice the goddamn thoughts on their stupid-ass lily pads. Okay, forget it. Clearly, this isn't working. Let's watch TV.

Jesus, Dr. Phil is a downer!

Alright, but I can't let this guy suck the life force out of me, there's a whole world out there to be seen and there are lives being lived. But he just kills me, this Dr. Phil. Today he's got these awesome fifteen-year-old kids on his show — these young people with hearts and heads still so brand-new and open to what's ahead of them — and he's doing his whole tough-love thing about how they need to have backup plans for their dreams, or how they have to perform academically or they can forget about playing music or sports and working at their dreams ever coming true, or some damn thing. And it's all hyped up for TV, of course, and these sweet kids are under lights with Doctor First Name getting them all worked up for good TV and it's just heartbreaking to watch.

I'm sitting here on the couch and I keep thinking about that play by Steve Martin called *Picasso at the Lapin Agile*. If Dr. Phil had ever shown up in Paris at the Lapin Agile in 1904 to have a drink with Einstein and Picasso, our twentieth century would've been screwed right then and there. Can you imagine?

PICASSO: "So you're saying you dream the impossible and put it into effect?"

EINSTEIN: "Exactly."

DR. PHIL: "I'll tell you what . . . you both better wake up and smell the coffee! Okay? Because I'll tell you something right now: all the hoopla pipe-dream load of horse-malarkey too-dle-doodle will not fly in the real world, okay? Listen to me for a minute instead of talking about 'Oh, the twentieth century has been handed to us so casually and it's staggering to be-lieve that we have sketched it out with pencils on napkins . . .' Sharpen that pencil, real good . . . okay? Pick it up. And start working on your SAT scores."

I see the tears welling up in this one teenager's eyes on screen. I'm sure some producer in the studio is really excited about this fact, and probably hoping for the cry that he thinks means good TV. At least we're lucky Dr. Phil didn't have a show when Wozniak, Jobs, Gates, and Allen were distracted from their homework and academic performance by dreams. Plus, the Dr. has a gut, and he wrote a diet book! *Hello?* If anything he should be honest and tell these kids, "Hey, I've got a forty-something-inch waist and a best-selling diet book, so obviously anything's possible. Just stay focused and out of trouble. You'll be fine, it's just a weird time any way you cut it, being sixteen." Anyway, I've switched off the TV, and I'm packing a suitcase because Maria and I are taking off tomor-row night. Goddamn, he's got another one of these kids on-stage and looking like he wants to give up. Way to go, Doc. Did Oprah give this guy his job? That seems ironic to me. Listen up teenagers of the world: stay away from Dr. Phil and keep your dream alive.

Alright, speaking of which, one week unemployed and I'm already sick of sitting around. I'm still alive, so I'm switch-ing off the TV and packing a suitcase. There's a whole world outside, and I've bought a decent stack of tickets to see some of it. First stop London, then up to Sweden, then out west to Los Angeles, up to San Francisco, back to New York to repack, and out west again and up into the Rocky Mountains. Then once winter starts, the last hurrah that's ticketed is the British Virgin Islands. Lest you think I'm another gazillionaire entertainment-industry fat cat or trust-fund brat, let me lay this interesting piece of accounting on you: How much do you spend partying with your friends after work at the local drinks-and-appetizers hole? Fifty bucks? A hundred? And how many nights a week? One? Three? Here's a trick: don't drink for eight years, put aside the drink tab money. Makes for a hell of a plane ticket and hotel fund. Anyway, the TV is off, the suitcase is packed, and life's clock is ticking away to time's cruel and indifferent little beat.

Hit it!

Exactly One Year After the Layoffs:
Hellhounds in God's Country

I'm trying to breathe very thin air while a team of twelve dogs is lurching, growling, barking, and pulling my jet-lagged body down a narrow, icy path at about nine thousand feet above sea level in the Colorado Rocky Mountains. While it feels like the type of lark that will certainly lead to personal injury or death, I am convinced I can somehow sell an article about dog sledding to a magazine somewhere down the line and pay my rent for a couple of months, so I am trying my best not to vomit or black out — as this will make for a better magazine article.

Behind the tether of haunches and fangs, Maria and I are crammed into a sled, and farther back, a man balances precariously on the sled's back rails, screaming commands in a language I can't understand, just inches behind and above my head. Words that might be Eskimo, for all I know. And at his loudest and most determined, it's as if he's afflicted with some kind of rash of tics, and he sounds something like a deaf man screaming a frustrated feeling at the top of his lungs. The commands show up in tight turns — strangely beautiful and loud, confident and discordant, these staccato stabs. The idea, I suppose, is that the dogs will hear that our man means business, and that'll keep them from heading straight for the ledge to my immediate right and plunging us to our deaths.

At the first slow part of the path, just after the initial downhill and hairpin turns, I get a chance to ask him how he found
himself with this job, or, more accurately, without a nine-to-
five office job. It turns out he has come by way of commercial
fishing in Florida. He was in a shipwreck there, though, so he
had a little downtime before he got here to Colorado. Lobster
boat went down. Sank with full traps onboard, but he lived.
Tore up his arm pretty good when it got stuck in some rigging, but nothing that didn't heal up with some injury pay
and a week or two of rest. Still, the adventure of barely es-
caping a sinking boat — stacked full with a half ton of angry
crustaceans — so he could come here and guide powerful dogs
through the rocky Mountains — seems practically biblical in
scale to me after my tame office job in the world of corporate
rock and roll. He says he has a girlfriend. Hell yes, he would
have to have a girlfriend! Who wouldn't, after that? You would
walk into the first bar, order a stiff shot, and explain to the
best-looking surfer girl there that you just escaped a sinking
ship stuffed and stacked with savage, angry, clawing monsters. You would casually go on about how you were going to
have a few drinks, rest up, then head to the Rockies and run
dog-sledding trips with a team of mongrels across frozen tun-
dra at ten thousand feet now that you've cheated death. Hell
yes, you would leave that bar with a girlfriend! As a matter of
fact, there would probably be two of them. And they would
be there with their sexually advanced, open-minded best
friend; the three of them hanging on your every word about
how you weren't afraid to be on a sinking ship out there at sea
that day.

He says that until the snow disappears in the spring thaw,
he's here running dogs, and then it will be off to the Pacific

Northwest, first for some well-earned rest, and then some commercial fishing for salmon or crab.

I look straight up from where I sit in the sled to the huge hanging walls and quiet, gigantic, almost lunar summits of the Rocky Mountains, and all I can think of are the lyrics to the new owner's romantic slow jam. How could he have said all of that stuff?

"I'll be waiting for you? Here inside my heart?" And then all the stuff about how he wants to be the one to love the listener/ me more than someone else can, and giving me everything I need. It's just not adding up.

Then my mind starts racing around the fact that I heard that one of the guys who used to run part of the label has a house somewhere around here, near Aspen. I actually crane my head around toward the back of the sled trying to get a better view of a huge house I thought I saw. My effort is noticed, probably for the pained grimaces and several loud grunts of determination that escape me when I try to turn my upper body and look behind us and way out to the other side of the canyon.

"Can I help you with something, there?"

"There's just this guy where I used to work has a house and . . . I'm trying to see . . . the . . ."

"That place across the canyon?"

"Yeah, this guy, uh, that I used to . . ."

"That's Michael Eisner's place. The Disney guy. He's never there though."

"Oh."

Goddamn. He's never there? You should see the size of the place! Seriously, larger than, like, a Safeway grocery store. I think everyone's figured this "success" thing out except for me. I should hijack this sled, yell at the dogs to make a hard right, get across this canyon and break into Eisner's house. Revolution!

"So, where do you two live?"

"New York," I say, hoping it makes me seem tough.

"What brings you out here?"

I sit thinking of a way to make the answer seem as romantic, fierce, and road-weary as it seems his life has been. Maybe I'll say something along the lines of, "Well, we've been clawing our way through New York City for the last seven or eight years, in the trenches . . . cockroaches . . . rats . . . had to get out of the greed race, just get in a car and drive. Ended up heading into the Rockies — gotta think about our next plan, since I got canned from my job and I'm not too into the idea of going back to living within some bullshit corporate structure." But what comes out is, "We live in New York and we flew in to go skiing with our friend Kim and, well, we had read about the dog sledding and thought we'd take a rest from skiing for a day and give it a try." Nice.

The dogs have slowed; you can feel that the speed-and-swerve honeymoon of hairpin turns has faded. This is the long haul that you knew somewhere inside of you certainly awaited, and their backs and legs settle into traversing terra firma in a stoop and hunch so familiar to their bones you realize they knew it was coming. Their haunches dig into a hardworking and predictable stride — the kind of gait that every living thing knows is required if you expect to last.

We talk a little to kill the time, and the guide says he's

thinking about maybe settling down sometime soon, that he knows he can't stay out on the road season-to-season forever. Says living that way has to end at some point. He starts asking us questions about what it's like to live in Manhattan. How many people have dogs? Do we think those people pay to have their dogs walked? How many would you say a guy could walk at once, how many total in the course of a day? He's crunching the numbers out loud, and figuring how it might be nice to settle down a little and make his money by taking walks in the park. The Colorado sun is going down. We keep on. Dogs, all of us.

Whole Lotta Love for Sale

Back home in New York and I'm waking up after flying in late last night. Maria is already off at work. I have to get some coffee. And some breakfast. Oh, and some work, so I can continue to enjoy stuff like electricity and food. For the last few weeks there have been headlines that the slow-jam-lyric-writing booze-magnate's grandson who bought the company is taking it public in an IPO that he hopes will raise well over half a billion dollars. I put on some shoes and hit the elevator. Our apartment is in a building located right across the street from the New York Stock Exchange, and when I get downstairs, I look up and see a huge blue flag flying with the Warner Music Group logo on it. Today's literally the day? Apparently. And any doubt is erased when I recognize the once-familiar music-biz motorcade of chauffeured black Mercedes sedans and see a stretch limo parked outside of the main entrance to the trading floor. Right now, behind those doors, they're cutting the company into 32.6 million pieces and hoping to sell them all.

Of the planned $750 million raised by today's IPO, the company's SEC filing is earmarking less than 1 percent of that — a mere $7 million — to be put toward the company's operations, with the rest going to pay down debt. But with the consortium having already been paid back more than their initial investment, word on the street is that the rest of the money will make for another round of pocket-lining like last year when, after posting a mere $7 million in operating income, the new owner paid out $22.5 million in salary and bonuses for the year . . . to the top five executives. This after firing over a thousand employees, not to mention cutting how many bands and artists from the company's roster of talent. Both the *Wall Street Journal* and the *New York Times* have run pieces this week about the band Linkin Park (35 million albums sold worldwide) begging out of their Warner Music Group contract on account of learning that only $7 million of the planned $750 million will be allocated to the company's day-to-day operations. To the band's credit, it speaks out publicly against the executives skimming millions and issues statements about the ethical shortcomings of the men who are whipping up this frenzy of what appears to be last-chance music-business looting. On a more level-headed note, they publicly question the company's ability to even operate effectively on a fiscal level given the kind of decisions that are being made. Linkin Park is quoted in the *Wall Street Journal* as saying, "We feel a responsibility to get great music to our fans. Unfortunately, we believe that we can't accomplish that effectively with the current Warner Music Group." The string section swells, David is taking on Goliath, and then . . . well . . . they, um, offer to stay if their contract is revised to pay out $60 million. I'm staring at the newspaper trying to figure out if this is simply a brilliant and subversive demand on behalf of the band, asking for the moon, knowing that they would never get it, so that they could get contractually released from a sinking ship. Jesus, the executives have cut over a thousand jobs then lined their pockets with seven-figure bonuses in the face of perpetually diminishing sales, and artists are offering to rethink flipping off the Man for an extra $45 million. Ah, rock and roll.

I keep walking past the line of black Mercedes Benzes, down Wall and into the Starbucks to grab something strong. Right next to the baked goods, on the counter next to the clerk's tip jar, there's a small display of CDs from some new band that I recognize as being signed to an imprint of Atlantic Records. Standing there, still kind of asleep, something finally occurs to me; something that arguably should have occurred to me when I was still being paid to think about selling CDs: do people even want to buy music in a physical format anymore? Then again, maybe this is the last remaining place on Planet Earth where somebody *would* buy a CD. After all, it's filled with adults like me already spending way too much on a product that they could get for a fraction of the price without leaving the comfort of their own home, but for whatever reason decide not to.

It's 11:00 AM, my ex-bosses are a block away, and by now they have somehow generated hundreds of millions of dollars by selling rock and roll to Wall Street when nobody is buying it at retail; when retail is going out of business.

Out the door, right in front of the stock exchange, I recognize the few usual clerks taking their smoke break outside. Suddenly, for no reason at all, a fat clerk with a beard sets his coffee down next to his foot on the ground, sticks his cigarette into the corner of his mouth, then starts clapping with his freed-up hands as he looks at the door to the stock exchange. It swings open and legendary Led Zeppelin guitarist Jimmy Page comes walking out in a suit and tie. For a minute I'm certain this isn't what's happening. Then another clerk starts clapping and in a thick Bronx accent says, "Yeah-yeah. Jimmmmmay!" This prompts the first guy, who has now picked his coffee back up, to take the cigarette out of the corner of his mouth and chime in with a thick New York and New Jersey salute, "Jimmy fawkin' Page." A photographer comes out of nowhere and starts to take aim with one of the many cameras around his neck. Page breaks into a move straight out of the seventies-rock-icon playbook: the short and fast zig-zagged dash to the limo, which I'm guessing is for the sake of a good action-packed photo, since there are no people or obstacles between him and the limo. My first thought when he zigs right, then zags left, is that I'm about to see a childhood rock-and-roll hero peppered with hot lead in a firestorm he unwittingly triggered with the kind of erratic movement that heavily armed SWAT officers and feds have been waiting to catch in their peripheral vision since September 12, 2001. Dude, easy with the sudden movements. I've got enough problems right now without your ass getting me nailed in the crossfire on my way home. I don't think I even have health insurance right now.

I look up at the armed officers guarding the Stock Exchange. They're wearing Kevlar vests and black riot helmets with face masks, and they have automatic rifles and ammo across their chests; but they're wearing the same slack-jawed amazed look as we all watch *the* Jimmy Page. I wonder if these guys used to sneak Led Zeppelin albums out of their sister's bedrooms, too, only to wind up here on this morning thirty years later. Page ducks into the limo fast and stays in there behind the dark black tinted glass. The door to the stock exchange swings open again, and this time a clean-cut-looking guy, in the same standard-issue Wall Street dark blue power suit that Page is wearing, comes walking out to the limo carrying two Gibson Les Paul guitars in cases. The limo trunk opens slowly, quietly, and mysteriously, and the guy loads the guitars into the trunk, closes it, and pats it with his hand, signaling to the driver that it's okay to go. It then takes the driver about six minutes to negotiate a very tight, backward and forward, lurching series of little three-point turns to get the limo heading in the right direction to exit the area, on account of the security blockades. Watching the driver slamming this long, fancy limousine into drive, then reverse, then drive, then reverse, and so on, all the while cranking the steering wheel hard to the right, hard to the left, makes Page's dash to get into the limo even more amusing in retrospect.

Back at the apartment I pour myself a bowl of cereal and put in the Led Zeppelin live DVD and watch the footage of them playing Madison Square Garden in 1975. Goddamn, look at them; this was the time before rock stars did advertisements. And these solos! These long, legendary guitar solos would never make it onto a rock record today. I think label executives today would shudder at the idea of interrupting another repetition of a radio-friendly chorus that they researched to death in focus groups and over telephones.

I'm sitting on a living-room floor, eating cereal and watching TV, staring at Jimmy Page, and it feels exactly the same as it did when I was nine. But this many years later I'm staring at Page in High Definition with 5.1 Surround Sound; a motion-picture version of the rock god on the poster I recall staring at on my bedroom wall when I was growing up. The coffee wakes me up enough to think, "Ten minutes ago I saw Jimmy Page on Wall Street in a suit and tie." It's not exactly the way I ever thought I'd bump into a member of the mighty Led Zeppelin in New York City. But it's not fair to expect the guy to stay the same, is it? This thing I'm doing here, it's a cheap shot, really. On the TV screen right now it's 1975, and Jimmy Page is playing like a man who answers to nobody. A man existing in that seductive state of extended adolescence that rock legends bask in, a man connected to something in the universe larger than even the sum total of the legendary Led Zeppelin, playing guitar because that is so clearly what he was put here to do. And it's wrong to expect that kind of divine moment to last forever, and to expect an artist to stay in 1975. Fact is, ten minutes ago I saw the guy onscreen right downstairs, coming off the trading floor of the stock exchange with a banker carrying his guitars for him. I sit cross-legged on the floor on a workday staring into my cereal bowl, thinking about how we all change. We all grow up. We all move on, one way or another, whether we want to or not.

THE END

LIMERICK
COUNTY LIBRARY

SUGGESTED FURTHER READING

The bathroom stall at the Continental,
according to Pat Carpenter

Flyers on telephone poles

Fine print in the contract

A decent map

SORRY, MA. FORGOT TO TAKE OUT THE TRASH:

BONUS TRACKS

My Six-Point System for Saving the Record Business

1. Rerelease CDs as "Very Deluxe Editions" — new packaging to include bonus DVD and two five-dollar bills.
2. Revise "Online Is a Fad" speech from 1999, 2000, 2001, 2002, 2003, 2004, and 2005 sales conferences. New title for speech will excite Wall Street: "Embracing Technology as We Rock into the Future."
3. Presidents and chairmen: If the last hit record you were responsible for was released over seven years ago, your new contract will be cut back to pay only $10 million for five years, plus bonuses, not to exceed $21 million total in salary and bonuses. Suck it up.
4. Top executives to maintain only two homes in North America, and only one in Europe.
5. Please note: If you use luxury helicopter charter service to get out to Hamptons to "See a band," please ask if anyone else plans on using a helicopter that evening, and try to helipool.
6. Overall: Adapt to getting by on 95 percent profit margin instead of 1,120 percent profit margin.

NEW YORK (AP) — It was a one-two encounter between Axl Rose and Tommy Hilfiger. The scuffle reportedly started after the Guns N' Roses front man moved the drink of Hilfiger's girlfriend, Dee Ocleppo. — Associated Press, Saturday, May 20, 2006

STOCKHOLM (Reuters) — Axl Rose, the lead singer of Guns N' Roses, was released from a Stockholm jail after 11 hours on Tuesday, Agence France-Presse reported. The police said that when he sobered up, he admitted to assaulting and biting a security guard in the lobby of his hotel and agreed to pay a fine of $5,430 and compensation of $1,360 to the guard. The incident took place after a concert and a night of partying. — *The New York Times*, June 28, 2006

FUTURE ODD DUSTUPS WE'D LIKE TO SEE FROM THE FORTY-FOUR-YEAR-OLD GUNS N' ROSES FRONTMAN

OMAHA (AP) — Axl Rose, frontman for Guns N' Roses, the nineties hard-rock band best known for hits like "Welcome to the Jungle," "Sweet Child o' Mine" and "Paradise City," was arrested downtown Friday night after repeatedly slapping the face and biting the ear of legendary 76-year-old multibillionaire investor Warren Buffett. Authorities said that after sobering up, Rose admitted he was "startled and confused" by Buffett. The scuffle took place in the lobby of Rose's downtown hotel, where the band and their crew were staying before moving westward on the U.S. leg of their current world tour.

DENVER (Reuters) — Guns N' Roses singer Axl Rose was treated for injuries at Eagle Valley Medical Center early Sunday morning after the 44-year-old rocker attempted to tackle a large black bear. After the band's Saturday night concert at the nearby Red Rocks Amphitheater, Rose was visiting friends in Vail when he saw the bear from the window of the lodge where he and his friends were drinking and enjoying a late-night private meal. After sobering up, Rose admitted that the incident was unprovoked but that "there was something about that bear." The band plays in Washington State tomorrow night.

SEATTLE (UPI) — Early-morning pedestrians had to wonder: Who was the man making monkey sounds and throwing food scraps from a paper sack at passerby early Tuesday morning in down-town Tacoma? The primate impersonator was none other than legendary Guns N' Roses singer Axl Rose, apparently blowing off some steam after a long night of partying that started when the band completed its concert at the Tacoma Dome the prior eve-ning. Authorities said Rose's actions were largely perceived as harmless and even entertaining by early-morning foot traffic, that is until the rocker-turned-monkey-man started threatening to bite people. Tacoma resident Clyde Drew said, "It was kind of funny at first. He would make monkey sounds and run around in little circles and it was kind of a little game, you had to get past him on the sidewalk before he could turn around and throw food at you from the sack that he was holding." Drew went on to say that the fun and games ended when Rose threatened to bite him and several other passersby. After sobering up, Mr. Rose agreed to pay a fine of $4,000 and commented, "I don't know what to say about this one. I don't know . . . we finished the show, I was backstage having a few beers with the guys, and I just thought to myself, 'This [expletive] town needs a little visit from Mr. Monkey

Rose and they're gonna get one before the night's over.'" This week's concert at the Tacoma Dome concludes the western U.S. leg of their world tour and the band will now head to New York and then London, where the European portion of their tour will commence.

The Most Important Thing Between Writer and Editor Is Open Communication

From: A. Fusco
To: Dan Kennedy
Subject: Re: Manuscript?

When can I expect manuscript? Been a while.
— A.

From: Dan Kennedy
To: A. Fusco
Subject: Re: Manuscript?

Threw it in river.
Plan to pay back advance with gift certificates to something called
Linens and Things from American Express Rewards program.

TITLES FOR THIS BOOK THAT WERE DISCARDED
AFTER FRIENDS SAID THEY SOUNDED MORE LIKE
MORRISSEY SONGS THAN BOOK TITLES

*We Sit in Expensive Chairs,
Guessing What Might Fascinate You*

Aim for the Iceberg and Speed Up

Do Not Disturb Nero

How We Are Rocking So Slowly

THE AUTHOR WISHES TO THANK
THE FOLLOWING PEOPLE

William Russell Kennedy and Lori Ann Kennedy for getting me here to earth and everything after. Maria Lilja for creative direction and humor and, and, and. Trish Kennedy for hanging out ever since my luckiest December, and Jerry Gonzaga for making us all laugh so damn hard and learn so much. Susanne Lilja, Hans Hjelmqvist — and the Stockholm, Katrineholm, and Vauxholm contingencies! Antonia Fusco and everyone at Algonquin. Jim Levine, Daniel Greenberg, Arielle Eckstut, and everyone at Levine Greenberg. Kassie Evashevski, Vicky Germaise, Lee Stimmel, James Lopez, Sara, Chip, Lou, Misty, Jill Kaplan, Phil Botti, David Burrier . . . all the good apples. Sabrina, your visit was a highlight in the best of ways.

John Warner, Jennifer Traig, Suzanne Kleid, and all at Timothy McSweeney's Internet Tendency, Wholphin, and 826 Valencia in San Francisco.

Raha Naddaf, David Stevenson, John Murphy, Eric Ahlquist, Ben and Janine, Joshua Wolf Shenk, Cameron and Sheri and King, Loren Victory, Nat and Marcy, Michael Belli, George Dawes Green, Gary Baseman, Lea Thau, Jenifer Hixson, Catherine Burns, Sarah Austin Jenness, Chris Stamey, Whitney Pastorek, Todd Hanson, Beth Lisick, Graham Hill, Kim Ludlow, Jerry Stahl, Jason Gordon, Ian Faith, Kevin Sampsell, Barb Klansnic Scot and Kerry Armstrong, Meirav Devash, Stephen Smith, Juan Carlos Restrepo, Billy Burke, Amy Maguire, Jesse Parry, Freak Storm, Jeff Freiert, Mark Katz, Dave Statman, Artie

Fufkin at Polymer, Doug Pepper, Dave Massey, Johnny Suede, Del Rae McLain-Evans, Ethan Watters, Joe "Smoke Gobbler" Ryder, Tom Mara at KEXP in Seattle, the Foors — Paul, Linda, Hunter, Jake, Chloe. Sam Chapin and Brian Syrdal, Harris Bloom, Adam Wade, Chris Wilson at a camp someplace past Forrest Ranch maybe, Kevin Smokler, John Atkins, Roman Mars, Chef Peter Morrison of Moxy and always from Chez Shea, and Shaun O'Dell and Jeff Anderson, both of whom I've spent too much time missing. *And what of Dan Holloway? Hello? You there, Holloway?*

CREDITS

Recorded in New York, London, Los Angeles, Stockholm, British Virgin Islands, Montana, Colorado, and Chico, California.

Produced by Sir David Walter "Knobs" Thomas IV
Engineered by Tim "Frankenstein's Tax Man" Kell
Assisted by Lim "Nickname" Nyphuk
Mixed and mastered by Antonia Fusco at Algonquin Books,
225 Varick Street, New York, New York.

Beats and string arrangements: Antonia Fusco, Maria Lilja,
Ben Whitten, Nat Whitten
Road crew: Kip, Slug, Mammy, and Rendang (Mascot: Taco)
Legal: Stern, Frank, White & Smug.
Ambassador of Fixing Everything at Any Point: Daniel Greenberg
Booking in North America: There is no booking agent for live
appearances North America

Booking in Europe: One of these is missing from the picture as well
REALLYSMALLTALK.COM HAS BEEN A SECRET SOCIETY SINCE 2002

This book was written to be read LOUD, so CRANK IT UP!

Questions Designed To Provoke Light Discussion Of Death,
Money, Love, Loneliness And Pop Music
A READING GROUP GUIDE FOR
Rock On: How I Tried to Stop Caring about Music
and Learn to Love Corporate Rock
by Dan Kennedy

1. What is it that makes Dan Kennedy (untraditionally) hand-some, interesting, an outdoor type, a good listener/nondrinker/nonsmoker? Female members of discussion group should break off into pairs and discuss.

2. How did you feel after reading *Rock On* and then discussing question number one and basically admitting that you would probably fall in love with Dan Kennedy if his current girlfriend reads this book, realizes he can't hold a job, and subsequently dumps him? For this one you simply e-mail your answer and contact information to dskmail@earhlink.net.

3. Do you know that these questions were written by a professional and not by Dan Kennedy and therefore aren't inappropriate or odd in that regard? Discuss.

4. Have you ever felt like you had to set yourself aside, almost became someone else, in order to succeed in an office environment? And did it leave you longing to simply get back to being the person you recall setting aside, the person who used to feel certain ways about the world outside and notice small details like, say, the way the light became perfect in your house when the windows were a little bit dirty and diffusing the morning

sun? Where did the *real* you go? Is it all just part of growing up? Is the world a place that requires a certain amount of discipline and effort from one who expects to continually see the small details and romance in the little day-to-day stuff, much less be inspired by it? Wait . . . what was the question again?

5. If you had to pick just three thousand MP3s to be stuck on a desert island with, what would those three thousand songs be? And give a reason why you chose each particular one when you read the titles of the songs to the discussion group.

6. As people, we veer so oddly between thinking it's too late for the likes of us and then in the next moment thinking we're at the beginning of it all. The answer to this one: True.

7. Okay, let's see . . . Would you consider starting a band late in life? Why is the act of playing music taken with such an ambitious careerist forethought by most people? Granted, it gets kind of sad when it's people, say, Dan Kennedy's age (dskmail@earthlink.net), drunk on sensible wine at a dinner party and someone decides, "Hey let's have a jam session and drink more wine!" But what would the crime be in forming a decent band at, for example, age thirty or forty or . . . ? Really, is that a crime? (Last part of question is rhetorical.)

8. In *Rock On* the new boss who was promoted to head of the department wore sunglasses in the morning marketing meeting. What's the most sort-of grossly and sadly ego-driven behavior you recall from a former boss at a day job?

9. Would you consider listening to the album *Engine* by Amer-

ican Music Club? Terrific. But be careful, it's kind of heavy, but it's almost funny how heavy and sad it gets. Don't take it too seriously, but, man, what a beautiful album from way back. Is it wrong to advocate albums that came out eighteen years ago? (Correct answer: No, it is nothing to be embarrassed about. Don't worry.)

10. There is more love and money in the world than you could ever imagine. There was a nature show once where this guy found a bluff in New Mexico where these snakes were mating. Swear to god, no exaggeration, there were easily a couple hundred thousand snakes in just the one little patch of the bluff that he was standing next to. They were stacked, like, four feet deep. Who could even imagine that many snakes, even if someone told you they had seen that many? Anyway, don't you think that's the way it is with love and money, too? Seriously, don't you think so? You know, like, there's so much of it and one just has to find it? This has nothing to do with the book, but, honestly, there must be an unbelievable amount of abundance in this world that we can't even imagine. Discuss this idea, but get back to talking about *Rock On* by Dan Kennedy at some point.

11. Damn. It's late. Is this all just crazy talk? It feels like, "Will it be weird now after this?"

12. Book groups and book clubs are important, though. Anything besides going to the office, coming home, going to the office, coming home, is an important use of time. It's amazing how little effort it takes to enrich our day-to-day lives. Read a book and schedule a time to meet and discuss it, and you're

ahead of, like, 80 percent of the populace in terms of mental stimulation. Um . . . let's see here, right . . . we need a question in this one. Okay, so: What was one thing you, uh, liked about the ending of *Rock On*? Break into pairs and discuss.

13. There's this Nappy Roots lyric that goes, "Peanut butter, string beans, what's fucking with that?" Sorry for the profanity, but that has got to be one of my favorite rap lyrics of all time. Is profanity necessary in expressing oneself? Would this lyric be nearly as fun, entertaining, sincere, without profanity? Like, would you rather it were left as is, or changed to one of the following:

A) Peanut butter, string beans, who's to say these foods are wrong in any way?
B) Peanut butter, string beans, hoorah.
C) Peanut butter, string beans (silence).